*"Information through Innovation"*

# The Programmer's Guide to the AS/400

**Robert W. Janson**

*Florida Community College
at Jacksonville*

bf

**boyd & fraser publishing company**

**Executive Editor**: James H. Edwards
**Production Manager**: Peggy J. Flanagan
**Production Services**: Books By Design, Inc.
**Compositor**: Gex, Inc.
**Interior Design**: Books By Design, Inc.
**Cover Design**: Kevin Meyers
**Manufacturing Coordinator**: Tracy Megison

© 1994 by boyd & fraser publishing company
A Division of South-Western Publishing Co.
One Corporate Place • Ferncroft Village
Danvers, Massachusetts 01923

International Thomson Publishing
boyd & fraser publishing company is an ITP company.
The ITP trademark is used under license.

This book is printed on recycled, acid-free paper that meets
Environmental Protection Agency standards.

Manufactured in the United States of America

**Library of Congress Cataloging-in-Publication Data**

Janson, Robert W.
  The programmer's guide to the AS/400 / Robert W. Janson.
    p.  cm.
  Includes index.
  ISBN 0-87709-260-5
  1. IBM AS/400 (Computer)--Programming.  I. Title.
QA76.8.I25919J37  1994
005.2'45--dc20

93-45257
CIP

1 2 3 4 5 6 7 8 9 10 KE 7 6 5 4 3

# *Contents*

| **Chapter 6** | **AS/400 Database Management**  87 |

| **Chapter 7** | **Security**  112 |

| **Appendix A** | **Scheduling and Monitoring Jobs**  120 |

**Appendix B**

## Alternative Programming Environments  *125*

# *Preface*

This book has been written as a supplemental guide for any programming course that uses the AS/400. The specific language texts on RPG/400, COBOL, C, and so on, try to avoid being programming environment specific since this would limit their applicability. However, anyone learning a programming language for the first time has the added challenge of learning the programming environment: how to save and compile a program, how to create data files and load test data, and the like. This task is often as daunting as learning the language itself. Therefore, this book has been written to be programming language nonspecific. It can supplement an RPG/400, COBOL, C, or any other AS/400 supported programming language course.

All programming examples are in CL and are very basic. In fact, the text would fit nicely into an "Introduction to Programming Theory" course, with CL as the introductory language.

This text is not intended as a general user introduction to the AS/400. Rather, it concentrates on the functions and features that programmers would use to perform their tasks. If a general introductory text is being sought (covering a wider range of general user subjects, such as Query/400, PC Support, and OfficeVision/400), may I suggest another of my books, *Introduction to the AS/400*, also published by Boyd & Fraser Publishing Company.

All screen references and exercises in this book are for Version 2 Release 2 of the AS/400 operating system.

As always, I would enjoy any feedback, comments, or suggestions from you, the readers, and wish to thank my support group— Brenda, Mom, and Dad.

*Robert W. Janson*
*Jacksonville, Florida*

# *Introduction*

**1**

## Overview

The AS/400 was built for application development. It has a programming environment that provides a series of tools to enable the programmer to easily develop, test, and maintain application programs. To access these utilities, the reader needs to become familiar with AS/400 terminology and the appearance of the AS/400 screens and menus. The AS/400's utilities are tied together with an extensive menu system. This chapter covers the basic screens and menus that allow users to sign on and access the AS/400. How to navigate through the system menus and how to use the extensive on-line help system are also discussed.

The AS/400 also has a unique storage structure. We will define the various types of storage entities, their purpose, and their interrelationships.

After finishing this chapter, you will understand:

- The relationship among libraries, objects, and members on the AS/400
- The general functions available through the two main programmer utilities, PDM and SEU

You also will be able to:

- Sign on to the AS/400
- Use the on-line help facility
- Access AS/400 functions through the menu system

# Accessing the AS/400 and Navigating the Menus

To access the AS/400, you need a *signon id* and a *password*. Unlike small systems where there is one user per system, the AS/400 is a multiuser system. Whenever more than one user is involved, a need for identification and security arises. If one user is the accountant in charge of payroll and another is a manager, they will both require and store different information on the machine (e.g., employee salary history vs. employee evaluations). There is a need to keep this information confidential and allow only authorized people to access this data. To provide this security, the AS/400 needs to be able to uniquely identify each user. This is achieved by giving each user a unique signon id and password. The AS/400 also provides an extensive security system (see Chapter 7) that correlates userids to the files and functions they are allowed to access and use.

To access the AS/400 from your workstation, bring up the AS/400 `Sign On` screen (Figure 1.1). (How to bring this up depends on your particular system and network configuration. If necessary, see your systems support representative for help.) At this screen enter your unique userid and password in the space to the right of the string of periods that follows the words `User` and `Password`. The password will not appear on the screen. (This prevents someone from seeing the password and gaining unauthorized entry into the system.) Press **ENTER**.

Under a basic system configuration, the `AS/400 Main Menu` screen should be displayed (Figure 1.2). If the `Main Menu` screen is not displayed, simply type **go main** at the command line. Toward the bottom of the `AS/400 Main Menu` screen, notice the symbol `===>` and the underscores to the right of it. The underscores mark the location of the command line. System commands can be entered here. The go main command tells the AS/400 to display the AS/400 `Main Menu`.

**FIGURE 1.1**

```
                            Sign On


                                   System. . . . . .:
                                   Subsystem . . . .: QINTER
                                   Display . . . . .:


           User . . . . . . . . . . .  _____
           Password . . . . . . . . .
           Program/procedure. . . . .  _____
           Menu . . . . . . . . . . .  _____
           Current library. . . . . .  _____







                         (C) COPYRIGHT IBM CORP. 1980, 1991.
```

**FIGURE 1.2**

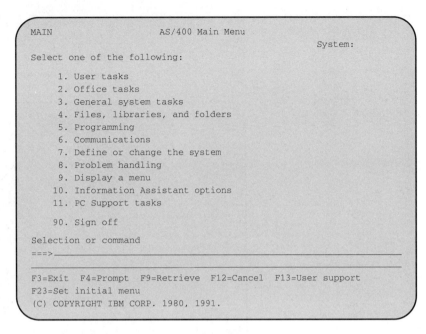

```
MAIN                        AS/400 Main Menu
                                                      System:
Select one of the following:

        1. User tasks
        2. Office tasks
        3. General system tasks
        4. Files, libraries, and folders
        5. Programming
        6. Communications
        7. Define or change the system
        8. Problem handling
        9. Display a menu
       10. Information Assistant options
       11. PC Support tasks

       90. Sign off

Selection or command
===>_____

F3=Exit  F4=Prompt  F9=Retrieve  F12=Cancel  F13=User support
F23=Set initial menu
(C) COPYRIGHT IBM CORP. 1980, 1991.
```

The go command is just one of many shortcuts that the AS/400 offers users to access screens and functions faster.

One method to get to the various AS/400 utilities is to choose options from each menu. You can do this by typing the option number at the command line and pressing ENTER. Each option will bring up another menu or screen. As options are chosen, you will progress through a series of submenus until the desired system function is reached.

Another way to execute a system function (and bypass the intervening screens) is to enter the correct CL command with the needed command information and press ENTER. This directly activates the system function. As you become more familiar with the AS/400, you will rely less on the menus and more on the commands. However, in the beginning, the menu system is a lifesaver.

## Using On-Line Help

Another important ease-of-use and learning feature of the AS/400 is its extensive on-line help facility. From any AS/400 screen, the user can press F1 for *contextual help*, which gives an explanation of the screen being viewed and the options and functions that can be chosen. For instance, pressing F1 at the AS/400 Main Menu screen will display the AS/400 Main Menu - Help screen (Figure 1.3). If the text More... appears in the bottom right-hand corner of the screen, it means there are further pages of information. Press PAGE DOWN to scroll through the information.

Another use of help is to find more information about system messages, which can be sent for various reasons. For instance, an incorrect system command may result in an error message. More often, the system sends informational messages regarding actions or the status of requests. Given the limited space available on screens, sometimes the messages are not totally clear about the seriousness of the error or its repercussions. An easy way to get more information on system messages is through contextual help. By moving the cursor to the message and pressing F1, a help screen will be displayed that explains the message in greater detail, gives possible reasons for the message, and suggests actions to resolve any problems. If the message still is not clear, the help information will often refer to other functions within the system or to system manuals that can provide more information.

**FIGURE 1.3**

```
MAIN                          AS/400 Main Menu
.....................................................................
  :                      AS/400 Main Menu - Help                    :
  :    The AS/400 Main (MAIN) menu allows you to select the general task :
  :    you want to do.                                             :
  :                                                                :
  : How to Use a Menu                                              :
  :                                                                :
  :    To select a menu option, type the option number and press Enter. :
  :    To run a command, type the command and press Enter. For assistance :
  :    in selecting a command, press F4 (Prompt) without typing anything. :
  :                                                                :
  :    For assistance in entering a command, type the command and press F4 :
  :    (Prompt). To see a previous command you entered, press F9   :
  :    (Retrieve).                                                 :
  :                                                                :
  :    To go to another menu, use the Go to menu (GO) command. Type GO :
  :    followed by the menu ID, then press the Enter key. For example, to :
  :                                                        More... :
  : F3=Exit help   F10=Move to top  F11=Search index  F12=Cancel   :
  : F13=User support F14=Print help                                :
.....................................................................
```

A second help feature is *index search*, which provides information by topic. Pressing **F11** at any help screen will bring up the Search Help Index screen (Figure 1.4). At this screen, type the topic or phrases to search for and press **F5**. For instance, type **pdm** and press **F5**. The result will be a list of topics related to the *program development manager* (Figure 1.5). To display the topic text, type **5** to the left of the topic title, under the Option heading, and press **ENTER**. The help information can also be printed by typing **6** next to the Topic title and pressing **ENTER**. The index search can be accessed from any help screen.

**FIGURE 1.4**

```
                        Search Help Index

    Index Search allows you to tell the system to search for specific
    information. To use Index Search, do the following:

     1. Type the phrase or words to search for.

     2. Press Enter.

    When you press Enter, the system searches for topics related to the
    words you supplied and displays a list of topics found.

    If you press Enter without typing anything, the system displays a list
    of all available topics.


    Type words to search for, press Enter.
      PDM _____

    F3=Exit help  F5=All topics  F12=Cancel  F13=User support
```

FIGURE 1.5

```
                    Main Help Index for AS/400

Type options, press Enter.
   5=Display topic     6=Print topic

Option  Topic
   _       Find string using PDM (FNDSTRPDM) command
   _       PDM (programming development manager)
   _       Start programming development manager (STRPDM) command
   _       Work with libraries using PDM (WRKLIBPDM) command
   _       Work with members using PDM (WRKMBRPDM) command
   _       Work with objects using PDM (WRKOBJPDM) command




                                                              Bottom
Or to search again, type new words and press Enter.
  PDM _____

F3=Exit help  F5=All topics  F12=Cancel  F13=User support
```

Another ease-of-use feature is the function key definition area on each AS/400 screen. The bottom two lines of every AS/400 screen identify and define the function keys allowed for that screen. This is a common feature found throughout the system and is just one more example of the common user interface that makes the AS/400 so user friendly. Some screens, however, cannot fit all of the function keys within those two lines. In that case, F24 will allow the user to scroll through the other function key definitions within that two-line area.

To exit from the AS/400, type **SIGNOFF** at the command line on any screen and press ENTER.

## Storing Information on the AS/400

The AS/400 operating system treats all stored entities (programs, files, documents, and so forth) the same—meaning that all entities are accessed and managed with the same commands. These entries reside in three primary storage items: *libraries*, *objects*, and *members*.

A library acts as an index or directory of related objects. Some objects, in turn, act as directories of members. Members contain source code, file definitions, or data.

Similar members are usually grouped within the same object and library. (For instance, the AS/400 has preexisting objects within library QGPL to group programs by the language they are written in: QRPGSRC for all RPG programs, QCBLSRC for COBOL programs, and so on.) Again, source code and file definitions are typed into members. These members are grouped within a special type of object that is meant to hold source code members. (There are a variety of different object and member types, which we will cover in more detail later in the chapter.) Objects, in turn, are organized into libraries.

To work with these various entities, the AS/400 has a utility called *PDM* (Program Development Manager), which provides a menu system that ties many common application development functions together. For instance, copying files is a commonly used function during application development. Programmers use a copied version of a data file to test their programs rather than possibly corrupt the original data. Also, when writing a program, programmers often start by copying a similar program's source code rather than reentering the duplicate code.

Files can be copied by typing in a CL command and specifying the names of the files to copy to and from (according to the command's syntax rules). Alternatively, PDM could be used to provide a list of all files within a library. The file to be copied can be picked from the list, and the user would type the name of the new file in a field provided by PDM. PDM would then build the correct CL command and submit it to be executed. By using PDM, knowledge of each command and its syntax is not required.

*SEU* (Source Entry Utility) is another useful programming tool. It provides a full-screen editor for programmers to create application programs. The editor has many of the same functions as a word processing application such as insert, delete, and search. It also supplies some specialized functions for programmers such as providing a prompt for programming language commands. Programmers would specify the programming language command they wished to enter, and SEU would supply a fill-in-the-blanks display where the appropriate variables and keyword parameter values could be entered. SEU also provides on-line syntax checking. As the programming language code is entered, the utility checks the validity of each line. The programmer does not have to run the program or wait for a compiled listing of the program to get syntax errors. The on-line syntax checker responds with error messages when the source code is entered into the file.

## Objects and Their Organization

The AS/400 has its own terminology regarding stored entities. As mentioned earlier, all information—programs, data files, data definitions, printer descriptions, and so on—is stored in libraries, objects, or members. Libraries are made up of objects, and some objects are made up of members. Other objects do not have members. A hierarchy or ownership relationship exists among libraries, objects, and members: A member must be in or belong to an object, and all objects belong to a library (Figure 1.6). When an object is referenced, the library it belongs to and the object name uniquely identify the object. When a member is referenced, the member's "owning" object and library are needed to clearly identify the member.

**FIGURE 1.6**

**The Hierarchical Relationship Among Libraries, Objects, and Members**

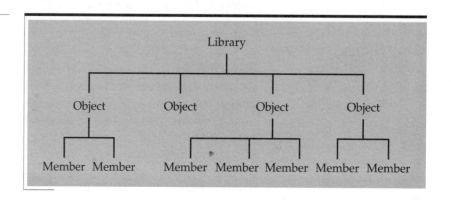

## Libraries

Libraries are used to group related objects. Libraries act as directories. For instance, in a programming environment, programs and the data they use are usually grouped within the same library (all the payroll programs and payroll files are stored within the same library, for example). Often, with large applications, there are also multiple copies of the same program. The copy being used day to day by the user is called the *production* copy. If the program is being modified or enhanced, the programmer uses a *development* copy. The initial code changes are made to the development copy. It is also used for initial testing until there is a successful compile and the program does not abend (abnormally end) when it is executed. Once the programmer has gotten the program to run, he or she usually creates a new copy called the *test* copy. A test copy is used to run against test data that simulates the real-world environment. After the logic of the program is successfully tested, the test version will be copied to create the new production version.

Having three versions of a program can make a programmer's life quite confusing. If there are three versions of every program, how do you remember which program is which? Imagine if there are hundreds or thousands of programs.

Libraries can help. Three libraries can be created: development, test, and production (Figure 1.7). You can initially create an object in the development library to hold the program. After the program has been entered or changes have successfully been made, the program from the development library can be copied to the test library. If during testing, problems are uncovered, the programmer can go back to the development version and rework the program. Then, when satisfied, the authorized person can copy the program back to the test library. After the program has been thoroughly tested, a copy would be sent to the production library, where it would be available to the users.

**FIGURE 1.7**

**Program Promotion Path Through Development, Test, and Production Libraries**

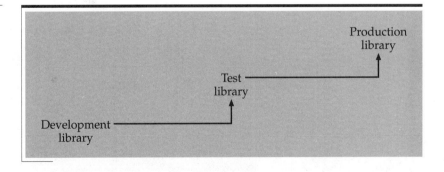

This is a common library organization for programs and data. Day-to-day, "real live" data is stored in production library data objects and members. A subset of the production data resides in the test library. This would spare the real data from any mistakes that might occur during testing yet still provide data that simulates the production environment. Finally, programmers could create data needed for initial testing and store it in the development library. Using the three different libraries, there is never a question of which program is which. Further, it is easier to control access to the production-level programs and data because they are all grouped together in one library.

# Objects and Members

Objects and members contain all AS/400 programs and data. Their relationship, however, is not very straightforward. Each kind of object or member has a different relationship to other kinds of objects or members. (The relationships are a little complex, but if you follow the text closely, study the diagrams, and go over it several times, they should become clear.)

Objects are characterized by a *type* and sometimes an *attribute* (Figure 1.8). Objects can have types equal to a variety of values. Some of the more common ones are *FILE, *PGM, and *MENU. Obviously, type values describe the information stored in the object. An attribute further describes objects that have a type of *FILE and some other objects that are the result of compiling a *source code member*. (A program is an example of a type of object created from compiling a source member.)

Examples of attributes for objects with a type of *FILE are *PF-SRC* and *PF-DTA*. PF-SRC means the file is a source physical file (Object1 in Figure 1.8). Members in a source physical file contain *source code*, which is a series of program language commands or data definition statements. All the members in Figure 1.8 (Larry, Curley, and Shemp) contain source code, which is why they reside under a source physical file, Moe. PF-DTA means the file is a data physical file (Figure 1.9). Members belonging to a data physical file contain data.

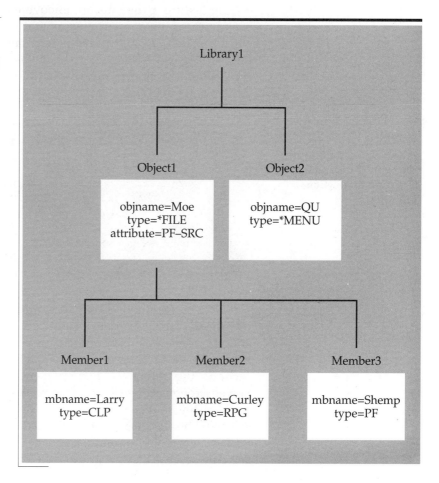

**FIGURE 1.8**

**Relationship of Source Physical Files and Members**

**FIGURE 1.9**

**An Example of Source Physical and Data Physical Files**

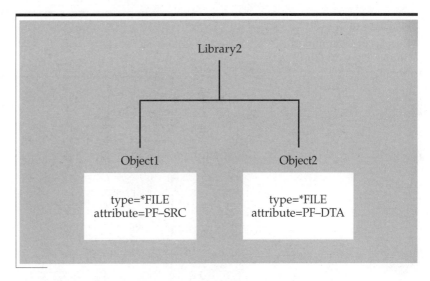

Members are classified by a *member type*. Member types and object types are different. The member type (CBL, CLP, RPG, PF) defines either the type of programming code contained in the member (COBOL, CL, RPG) or that the member is a physical file definition (PF) and contains DDS (*Data Description Specification*) statements, which define a file.

Members (such as Larry, Curley, and Shemp in Figure 1.8) in an object with an attribute of PF-SRC (such as Moe) contain source code instructions. Source code instructions are typed in by programmers and are "human readable." Computers cannot execute source code instructions; they execute machine language instructions. Compiling source code on the AS/400 converts source code into machine language instructions.

When a source code member is compiled, the system creates an object, and the compiled code is placed in that object. (In some other computer architectures, this machine code would be called a *load module* or an *executable file*.) This new object, created by compiling source code contained in a member, is defined by the system with a type equal to *PGM. Its attribute is dictated by the member type from which it was compiled. For instance, an object with an attribute of CLP (such as Object4, Larry, in Figure 1.10) is created when a member with type of CLP (Member1, Larry in Figure 1.10) is compiled.

When a member with a type of PF (such as Shemp) is compiled, a new object and a new member are created (see Object3 and Member4 in Figure 1.10). The new object's type is defined as *FILE, and its attribute is set to PF-DTA. The new member that is created does not have a type.

Using PDM to compile members Larry, Curley, and Shemp (which is not nearly as painful as some of the things Moe did to each of them) would result in three new objects and one new member (see Figure 1.10).

Object4 (Larry) is the result of compiling Member1 (Larry). Object5 (Curley) is the result of compiling Member2 (Curley). The third object and the fourth member, both named Shemp, are the result of compiling Member3, Shemp. The new object, Shemp, contains the machine language version of the file definition, and the new member will eventually hold the file's data. Notice also that Member4 has no type. Members belonging to a data physical file, by definition, contain data and have no type. You can see, from Figure 1.10, all the naming conventions for the new objects and members and their associated attributes and types.

**FIGURE 1.10**

**Results of Compiling Source Physical File Members**

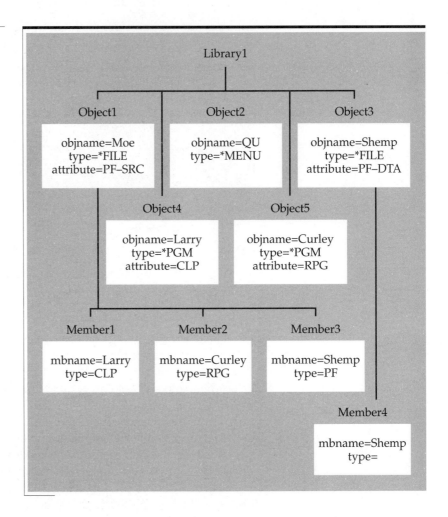

To write a program, a library, object, and member must be created. As mentioned earlier, system functions (such as creating libraries or objects) can be performed through PDM or by issuing operating system commands directly. Application programs communicate with the operating system through an *API* (Application Program Interface). There are IBM-supplied APIs for many of the AS/400 system functions, and the operating system is no exception. OS/400's API is a set of operating system commands (CL commands) that can be issued directly by application programs. These commands allow the application programs to interact with the computer hardware through operating system programs. By using the API, the applications are buffered from any hardware changes. If hardware changes required operating system program changes, the API commands would stay the same. This would allow application programs to continue running on the new hardware with no changes or recompiling.

Users can execute a wider range of operating system functions by directly typing in CL commands at any command line. Usually, AS/400 beginners prefer the menus and screens because they don't have to memorize commands, parameter keywords, and their syntax. The screens also serve as very good learning tools by clearly showing all available options and values. As you become more familiar with the individual CL commands, however, you will want to save time by just typing them in at the command line rather than paging through prompt screens.

Application programs cannot contain all the CL commands that can be directly executed from the command line. However, application programs can access these other commands because CL commands can be batched and then called by application programs. A programmer can create a CLP (Control Language Program) that contains CL commands that are not executable from within an application program. This new CLP can be called by the application program and data passed between the application program and the called CLP. Through passed data, the application program can control the execution of operating system functions. Conversely, the system commands' returned results can be used in further processing by the application program. We will cover CL in more detail in later chapters.

## Summary

The AS/400 is very easy to use. There are a variety of ways that users can access and use AS/400 functions. The menu system, on-line help (both contextual and index search), and the APIs each provide a different method for the user to access and understand the available system functions.

PDM and SEU provide easy access to often-used programming functions. Everything from creating and loading source code members to deleting libraries can be done within the screens and functions provided by these two utilities.

The AS/400 also has a programming object structure that provides a clear and uniform means for programmers to organize their programs and data. There are still procedures and authorizations that need to be instituted to provide an effective and secure programming environment, but the object-oriented nature of the AS/400 provides the basis for this organization.

## LAB EXERCISE

In this lab exercise, you will use the on-line help facility. Specifically, you will use the index search to find information on specific topics and message help to diagnose an incorrect command.

1.  Sign on to the AS/400.
2.  From any screen, press F1 to invoke help.
3.  Press F11 to select the index search option.
4.  Type the first item in Review Question 1 (Source Entry Utility) and press ENTER.
5.  Print the first topic by selecting option 6.
6.  Perform steps 3 through 5 for the other utilities contained in Review Question 1.
7.  Exit help by pressing F3.
8.  At the command line, type an incorrect command (for example, **STRMDP**) and press ENTER.
9.  Move the cursor to the message at the bottom of the screen.
10. Press F1 to invoke message help.

11.  Notice the error message's unique message ID and the possible reasons that the error occurred.

12.  Print the error message by pressing F1, the Print or Print Screen key.

## REVIEW QUESTIONS

1.  Describe the types of functions provided by the following utilities:

    Source Entry Utility

    Program Development Manager

    contextual help

    index help

2.  Define the relationship between libraries, objects, and members.

3.  What is the purpose of maintaining separate development, test, and production libraries?

4.  How are objects characterized?

5.  What type of information do members of source physical files contain?

6.  What is the difference between a file with an attribute of PF-DTA and a file with an attribute of PF-SRC?

7.  What is the result of compiling an object?

8.  How are member types and object attributes related?

## DISCUSSION QUESTIONS

1.  Discuss the path a program travels through the development, test, and production libraries. What events cause the program to be moved between the different libraries?

2.  If the members in the following diagram were compiled using PDM, what would be the resulting object and member names, types, and attributes?

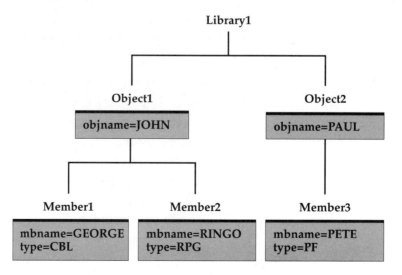

# PDM and SEU

## 2

## Overview

PDM and SEU are two utilities that provide easy access to programming functions heavily used during system development and maintenance. Creating, copying, deleting, and updating files as well as editing, compiling, and running programs can be easily accomplished through a series of menus, screens, and line commands provided by these programming aids.

This chapter covers some of the basic functions provided by PDM and explains how to create programs and execute them. A step-by-step walkthrough of the PDM screens and individual SEU line commands is also included.

After finishing this chapter, you will understand:

- The functions available through PDM
- The capabilities of SEU

You also will be able to:

- Access and navigate the PDM screens
- Create libraries and source physical file objects
- Create, input, edit, and compile a source member

## Starting PDM

As mentioned, PDM allows users to create and manipulate objects. This includes creating all the programming objects mentioned in Chapter 1, entering program source code and data definitions, and compiling the source code members. In addition, PDM allows you to save, modify, and delete objects.

To start PDM from the AS/400 Main Menu (see Figure 1.2), choose option 5, Programming, and press ENTER. This will bring up the Programming menu (Figure 2.1). From the Programming menu, select option 2, Programming Development Manager (PDM), and press ENTER. The PDM main menu (Figure 2.2) will appear.

If you are not at the AS/400 Main Menu screen, the AS/400 Programming Development Manager (PDM) menu can be accessed from any system screen by typing the CL command **STRPDM** (start PDM) at the command line and pressing ENTER.

The PDM main menu has options to work with libraries, objects, or members. Whenever one of these options is chosen, a screen will be displayed that asks for the library, object, or member with which to work. For identification of a member, the object and library names that it resides under are also requested. Members in different objects or different libraries can have the same name. If a member's library and object are not specified, the system will either use a default library and object name or search through the user's libraries and objects and select the first member that has the specified name. Unless the defaults are correct or the search order will yield the correct member, it's usually a good practice to fully describe the particular member by naming its library and object. The same holds for objects. When you identify an object, the library that contains the object should also be explicitly specified.

**FIGURE 2.1**

```
PROGRAM                     Programming
                                                    System: CHICAGO
Select one of the following:

     1.  Programmer menu
     2.  Programming Development Manager (PDM)
     3.  Utilities
     4.  Programming language debug
     5.  Structured Query Language (SQL) pre-compiler
     6.  Question and answer
     7.  IBM product information
     8.  Copy screen image
     9.  Cross System Product/Application Execution (CSP/AE)

    50.  System/36 programming

    70.  Related commands

Selection or command
===>

F3=Exit  F4=Prompt  F9=Retrieve  F12=Cancel  F13=User support
F16=AS/400 Main Menu
```

**FIGURE 2.2**

```
            AS/400 Programming Development Manager (PDM)

Select one of the following:

        1. Work with libraries
        2. Work with objects
        3. Work with members

        9. Work with user-defined options




Selection or command
===>_____
     _____

F3=Exit      F4=Prompt      F9=Retrieve      F10=Command entry
F12=Cancel  F18=Change defaults
```

## Creating Libraries and Objects

The AS/400 comes with many libraries already created, such as QGPL, which all users are allowed to access. Objects and members can be stored in these general-purpose libraries; however, as applications grow and as work on the AS/400 becomes more complex, programmers and users discover a need for individual members and objects. Before programs can be loaded in members and objects, the members and objects have to be created. And before members or objects can be created, a library must exist to hold them.

To create a library, choose option 1, Work with libraries, from the AS/400 Programming Development Manager (PDM) menu (see Figure 2.2). The Specify Libraries to Work With screen (Figure 2.3) will be displayed. If the library already existed, the user could

**FIGURE 2.3**

```
                    Specify Libraries to Work With

Type choice, press Enter.

   Library . . . . . . . *ALL____   *LIBL, name, *generic*, *ALL,
                                    *ALLUSR, *USRLIBL, *CURLIB












F3=Exit  F5=Refresh  F12=Cancel
```

work with it by typing in the library name at the library prompt (where the default value *ALL is located). For our purpose, accept the default prompt value *ALL, and press ENTER. A list of all the libraries that the user can access is displayed (Figure 2.4). Notice on the Work with Libraries Using PDM screen that options can be entered next to the libraries' names. These options direct the AS/400 to perform various functions, such as delete the library or display the library description.

**FIGURE 2.4**

```
                    Work with Libraries Using PDM

List type . . . . . . . *ALL_____     Position to . . . . . _____

Type options, press Enter.
   2=Change        3=Copy                   4=Delete   5=Display
   7=Rename        8=Display description    9=Save     10=Restore...


Opt  Library     Type        Text
 __   QGPL        *PROD




                                                              More...
Parameters or command
===>_____
F3=Exit      F4=Prompt        F5=Refresh      F6=Create
F9=Retrieve  F10=Command entry  F23=More options  F24=More keys
```

The function keys are another way to perform library tasks. Each key and its definition is listed at the bottom of the screen.

For our example, press F6 to create a library. Pressing F6 will result in the Create Library screen being displayed (Figure 2.5). At this screen, the name of the new library should be specified.

For all examples in this book, it is assumed that each user has a seven-character userid where the last two digits are a unique number, such as INTRO99. For the new library name, enter the text YOURLIB followed by the unique two-digit number. For userid INTRO99, the library name would be YOURLIB99. (The library name used in all examples will be YOURLIBXX, where XX is assumed to be the unique two-digit userid number.)

At the Create Library screen, descriptive text for this library can be entered. After specifying the new library, press ENTER. Pressing ENTER tells the system to start creating the new library. When the library is created, the Work with Libraries Using PDM screen will be redisplayed with a message on the second to last line saying Library YOURLIBXX created and YOURLIBXX will be included in the list of libraries (Figure 2.6). To verify that the library was actually created, find YOURLIBXX in the list. (You may have to scroll down the list of libraries.)

Now that a library exists, an object can be created. From the AS/400 Programming Development Manager (PDM) menu (see

**FIGURE 2.5**

```
                        Create Library (CRTLIB)

  Type choices, press Enter.

  Library. . . . . . . . . . . . .   YOURLIBXX_   Name
  Library type . . . . . . . . . .   *PROD        *PROD, *TEST
  Text 'description' . . . . . . .[*BLANK]_____
  _____




                                                              Bottom
  F3=Exit  F4=Prompt  F5=Refresh  F10=Additional parameters  F12=Cancel
  F13=How to use this display     F24=More keys
```

**FIGURE 2.6**

```
                     Work with Libraries Using PDM

  List type . . . . . . .  *ALL_____   Position to . . . . .  _____

  Type options, press Enter.
     2=Change       3=Copy                 4=Delete    5=Display
     7=Rename       8=Display description  9=Save     10=Restore ...

  Opt   Library    Type    Text

  __    QGPL       *PROD
  __    YOURLIBXX  *PROD




                                                             More...
  Parameters or command
  ===>_____
  F3=Exit      F4=Prompt        F5=Refresh        F6=Create
  F9=Retrieve  F10=Command entry  F23=More options  F24=More keys
  Library YOURLIBXX created.
```

Figure 2.2), choose option 2, `Work with objects`. This time the
`Specify Objects to Work With` screen (Figure 2.7) will be displayed. On this screen, specify the library under which the new
object will reside. For our example, type **YOURLIBXX** at the prompt
and press **ENTER**. This will bring up all objects contained in the
specified library (Figure 2.8). Since the library was just created, no
objects will be listed.

**FIGURE 2.7**

```
                 Specify Objects to Work With
Type choices, press Enter.

    Library. . . . . . . . . . YOURLIBXX_  *CURLIB, name

    Object:
      Name . . . . . . . . . *ALL_____  *ALL, name, *generic*
      Type . . . . . . . . . *ALL_____  *ALL, *type
      Attribute. . . . . . . *ALL_____  *ALL, attribute, *generic*,
                                          *BLANK




F3=Exit  F5=Refresh  F12=Cancel
```

**FIGURE 2.8**

```
                 Work with Objects Using PDM

Library . . . . . YOURLIBXX_  Position to. . . . . . . . _____
                              Position to type . . . . . _____

Type options, press Enter.
   2=Change         3=Copy       4=Delete    5=Display      7=Rename
   8=Display description          9=Save     10=Restore     11=Move ...

Opt  Object      Type    Attribute    Text

   (No objects in library)




Parameters or command
===>_____
F3=Exit       F4=Prompt         F5=Refresh        F6=Create
F9=Retrieve   F10=Command entry F23=More options  F24=More keys
```

But objects can be created from the Work with Objects Using PDM screen. Pressing F6 will bring up the Create Commands screen (Figure 2.9). This screen lists options to create a multitude of different types of objects. To decide which type of file to create, remember that the file we want to create will eventually hold a CL program and that the previous section on object types stated that all source code members must reside under an object with a type of *FILE and an attribute of PF-SRC (source physical file). Given these conditions, option 126 will create the type of object we want. (Paging down through the list of options will eventually result in the Create Commands screen, as shown in Figure 2.10, being displayed.) Typing 126 at the command line and pressing ENTER will bring up the Create Source Physical File (CRTSRCPF) screen (Figure 2.11). On this screen,

**FIGURE 2.9**

```
 CMDCRT                   Create Commands
 Select one of the following:
   Commands
        1.  Create Alert Table                        CRTALRTBL
        2.  Create APAR                               CRTAPAR
        3.  Create Authority Holder                   CRTAUTHLR
        4.  Create Authorization List                 CRTAUTL

        6.  Create BEST/1 Model                       CRTBESTMDL
        7.  Create Calendar                           CRTCAL
        8.  Create COBOL Program                      CRTCBLPGM
        9.  Create Configuration List                 CRTCFGL
       10.  Create C Locale Description               CRTCLD
       11.  Create CL Program                         CRTCLPGM
       12.  Create Class                              CRTCLS
       13.  Create Command                            CRTCMD
                                                            More...
 Selection or command
 ===>_____

 _____
 F3=Exit   F4=Prompt   F9=Retrieve   F12=Cancel   F16=Major menu
```

**FIGURE 2.10**

```
 CMDCRT                   Create Commands
 Select one of the following:
      116.  Create Save File                          CRTSAVF
      117.  Create Subsystem Description              CRTSBSD
      118.  Create Search Index                       CRTSCHIDX
      119.  Create Spelling Aid Dictionary            CRTSPADCT
      120.  Create SQL C Program                      CRTSQLC
      121.  Create SQL COBOL Program                  CRTSQLCBL
      122.  Create SQL FORTRAN Program               CRTSQLFTN
      123.  Create SQL Package                        CRTSQLPKG
      124.  Create SQL PL/I Program                   CRTSQLPLI
      125.  Create SQL RPG Program                    CRTSQLRPG
      126.  Create Source Physical File               CRTSRCPF
      127.  Create Session Description                CRTSSND
      128.  Create S/36 COBOL Program                 CRTS36CBL
      129.  Create S/36 Display File                  CRTS36DSPF
                                                            More...
 Selection or command
 ===>126_____

 _____
 F3=Exit   F4=Prompt   F9=Retrieve   F12=Cancel   F16=Major menu
```

enter the name of the new object, **CLOBJECT**, the library it will reside under, **YOURLIBXX**, and any descriptive text. After you do this, press **ENTER**. The system will start creating the new object. When it is complete, the Create Commands screen will reappear with a message at the bottom of the screen that says File CLOBJECT created in library YOURLIBXX. To verify that the object was created, go through PDM and get to the Work with Objects Using PDM screen for YOURLIBXX. It should display one object in that library, CLOBJECT (Figure 2.12), with an attribute of PF-SRC and a type of *FILE.

You are now ready to create a member.

**FIGURE 2.11**

```
                  Create Source Physical File (CRTSRCPF)

Type choices, press Enter.

File . . . . . . . . . . . . . .   CLOBJECT__   Name
  Library. . . . . . . . . . .       YOURLIBXX_  Name, *CURLIB
Record length. . . . . . . . .    92____        Number
Member, if desired . . . . . .    *NONE____     Name, *NONE, *FILE
Text 'description' . . . . . .     THIS IS A SOURCE PHYSICAL FILE
EXAMPLE_____



                                                               Bottom
F3=Exit  F4=Prompt  F5=Refresh  F10=Additional parameters  F12=Cancel
F13=How to use this display      F24=More keys
```

**FIGURE 2.12**

```
                  Work with Objects Using PDM

Library . . . . . YOURLIBXX_   Position to. . . . . . . _____
                              Position to type . . . . . _____

Type options, press Enter.
  2=Change      3=Copy      4=Delete    5=Display      7=Rename
  8=Display description  9=Save    10=Restore     11=Move ...

Opt Object   Type   Attribute Text
 _   CLOBJECT *FILE  PF-SRC    THIS IS A SOURCE PHYSICAL FILE EXAMPLE




                                                               Bottom
Parameters or command
===>_____
F3=Exit        F4=Prompt         F5=Refresh         F6=Create
F9=Retrieve  F10=Command entry  F23=More options  F24=More keys
```

## Creating a Member

To create a member, choose option 3, Work with members, from the AS/400 Programming Development Manager (PDM) menu. This will display the Specify Members to Work With screen (Figure 2.13), which prompts for the library and source physical file that will contain the member. Type the previously created library and object names, and press ENTER.

FIGURE 2.13

```
                    Specify Members to Work With
 Type choices, press Enter.

    File. . . . . . . . . CLOBJECT__    Name, F4 for list
      Library . . . . . .   YOURLIBXX_  *LIBL, *CURLIB, name

    Member:
     Name . . . . . . . . . *ALL_____   *ALL, name, *generic*
       Type . . . . . . . . *ALL_____   *ALL, type, *generic*, *BLANK












 F3=Exit   F4=Prompt   F5=Refresh   F12=Cancel
```

The `Work With Members Using PDM` screen (Figure 2.14) will
be displayed. This screen lists all the current members within the file
and provides a variety of member functions. To create a member,
press **F6**. The `Start Source Entry Utility (STRSEU)` screen will
be displayed (Figure 2.15). At this screen, the member name and type
to be created should be specified. For our example, create a member
called PGMMEMBER. Since a CL program will eventually be entered,
the member type would have to be CLP. To find out what values can
be entered in a prompt field, move the cursor to the field and press **F4**.
A help screen will be displayed with all the valid values. Doing this
for the `Source Type` prompt would result in the `Specify Value
for Parameter TYPE` screen (Figure 2.16).

FIGURE 2.14

```
                    Work with Members Using PDM
 File  . . . . . .  CLOBJECT__
   Library . . . .   YOURLIBXX_   Position to . . . . .  _____

 Type options, press Enter.
   2=Edit      3=Copy      4=Delete  5=Display  6=Print
   7=Rename    8=Display description  9=Save     13=Change text ...

 Opt Member    Type        Text

   (No members in file)





 Parameters or command
 ===>_____
 F3=Exit       F4=Prompt        F5=Refresh       F6=Create
 F9=Retrieve   F10=Command entry  F23=More options  F24=More keys
```

**FIGURE 2.15**

```
                    Start Source Entry Utility (STRSEU)

Type choices, press Enter.

Source file . . . . . > CLOBJECT      Name, *PRV
  Library . . . . . .   YOURLIBXX     Name, *LIBL, *CURLIB, *PRV
Source member . . . . . PGMMEMBER     Name, *PRV,  *SELECT
Source type . . . . . . *SAME_____    Name, *SAME, BAS, BASP, C...
Text 'description'. . . *BLANK_____




                                                                  Bottom
F3=Exit F4=Prompt F5=Refresh F12=Cancel F13=How to use this display
F24=More keys
```

The member type, CLP, could also be entered from this screen.
Entering **CLP** and pressing **ENTER** would bring back the Start
Source Entry Utility (STRSEU) screen with the type prompt
filled in with CLP. As can be seen in Figure 2.16, quite a variety of
types are available. If after viewing the valid options, you are still
unsure, move the cursor to the field and press **F1** for a list of all the
valid options and an explanation for each.

**FIGURE 2.16**

```
                    Specify Value for Parameter TYPE

Type choice, press Enter.

   Type . . . . . . . . . . . . . . :   SIMPLE NAME
   Source type. . . . . . . . . .       *SAME_____

   *SAME                                DSPF
   BAS                                  FTN
   BASP                                 ICFF
   C                                    LF
   CBL                                  MENU
   CICSCBL                              MNU
   CICSMAP                              MNUCMD
   CISCSQLCBL                           MNUDDS
   CL                                   PAS
   CLD                                  PF
   CLP                                  PLI
   CMD                                  PNLGRP
   DFU                                  PRTF                         +

F3=Exit F5=Refresh F12=Cancel F13=How to use this display F24=More keys
```

After the member type has been specified and descriptive text
has been entered, press **ENTER**. This will automatically invoke SEU,
and the Edit screen (Figure 2.17) will be displayed. This screen

**FIGURE 2.17**

```
Columns . . . :  1 71                  Edit                    YOURLIBXX/CLOBJECT
SEU==> _____PGMMEMBER
FMT ** ...+... 1 ...+... 2 ...+... 3 ...+... 4 ...+... 5 ...+... 6 ...+... 7
          *************** Beginning of data ********************************
''''''
''''''
''''''
''''''
''''''
''''''
''''''
''''''
''''''
''''''
''''''
''''''
''''''
''''''
''''''
          ****************** End of data **********************************
F3=Exit  F4=Prompt  F5=Refresh  F9=Retrieve  F10=Cursor
F16=Repeat find     F17=Repeat change        F24=More keys
Member PGMMEMBER added to file YOURLIBXX/CLOBJECT.                          +
```

allows the user to enter the program source code using SEU editing commands. We will cover SEU in another section, so for right now press **F3** to exit the edit function. The Exit screen (Figure 2.18) will be

**FIGURE 2.18**

```
                                    Exit

 Type choices, press Enter.

   Change/create member . . . . . . N           Y=Yes, N=No
     Member . . . . . . . . . . . . PGMMEMBER_  Name, F4 for list
     File . . . . . . . . . . . . . CLOBJECT__  Name, F4 for list
       Library. . . . . . . . . .      YOURLIBXX_ Name
     Text . . . . . . . . . . . . . CL_PROGRAM_ EXAMPLE_____
_____
   Resequence member . . . . . . . Y           Y=Yes, N=No
     Start . . . . . . . . . . . . 0001.00     0000.01-9999.99
     Increment . . . . . . . . . . 01.00       00.01-99.99

 Print member . . . . . . . . . . N           Y=Yes, N=No

 Return to editing. . . . . . . . N           Y=Yes, N=No

 Go to member list. . . . . . . . N           Y=Yes, N=No


 F3=Exit   F4=Prompt   F5=Refresh   F12=Cancel
```

displayed. This screen requires a confirmation that the member should be created. Entering **Y** at the Change/create member prompt and pressing **ENTER** directs the AS/400 to create the member. The Work with Members Using PDM screen will be displayed, and the newly created PGMMEMBER member with a type of CLP will be listed (Figure 2.19).

FIGURE 2.19

```
                    Work with Members Using PDM

     File . . . . . .  CLOBJECT__
        Library. . . .    YOURLIBXX_          Position to . . ._____

     Type options, press Enter.
       2=Edit      3=Copy      4=Delete  5=Display 6=Print
       7=Rename    8=Display description  9=Save     13=Change text ...

     Opt Member    Type        Text
      __  PGMMEMBER CLP_____     CL_PROGRAM_EXAMPLE_____



                                                              Bottom
     Parameters or command
     ===>_____
     F3=Exit      F4=Prompt        F5=Refresh        F6=Create
     F9=Retrieve  F10=Command entry  F23=More options  F24=More keys
     Member PGMMEMBER added to file YOURLIBXX/CLOBJECT.            +
```

## Manipulating Libraries, Objects, and Members

To perform a global operation on any of these storage entities, such as create, display, or delete, go through the Work with xxxxx screen (where xxxxx is libraries, objects, or members) and choose the appropriate function key or option to create, display, or delete.

As mentioned earlier, these options and functions can be executed directly from any system screen by entering the correct CL command on the command line. The correct command is often included at the end of a PDM screen's header enclosed in parentheses (see Figure 2.11). There is also a series of screens listing the types of CL commands and the commands themselves. These screens enable the user to zero in on the desired CL command by function, object type, and so on. We will cover more about how to find and invoke CL commands in Chapter 3.

## Starting SEU

As already shown, SEU is automatically invoked whenever a source physical file member is created. If the member has already been created, SEU can be activated to reedit the member. To invoke SEU, bring up the Work with Members Using PDM screen (see Figure 2.14) for the member to be edited. To the left of the member name type 2, the Edit option, and press ENTER. The SEU Edit screen (Figure 2.20) will be displayed.

SEU can also be started by typing STRSEU at the command line on any screen. The last member worked with will be chosen for editing.

**FIGURE 2.20**

```
     Columns . . . :  1  71              Edit           YOURLIBXX/CLOBJECT
     SEU==> _____PGMMEMBER
     FMT **...+... 1 ...+... 2 ...+... 3 ...+... 4 ...+... 5 ...+... 6 ...+... 7
          ***************** Beginning of data ***************************
          ******************** End of data ******************************
```

```
     F3=Exit    F4=Prompt   F5=Refresh   F9=Retrieve   F10=Cursor
     F16=Repeat find        F17=Repeat change          F24=More keys
```

## Using SEU

When a member is first created, it is empty. This is indicated by the Beginning of data and End of data lines following each other on the SEU Edit screen. SEU provides three different ways to execute edit commands: entering commands at the SEU command line (the second line on the left-hand side of the screen) and pressing ENTER; pressing function keys; or issuing line commands.

Line commands are entered to the left of the member line to be worked on. For instance, to insert five blank lines in the member, type I5 to the left of the Beginning of data line and press ENTER. The result would appear as in Figure 2.21, which shows five blank lines preceded by ''''''''. As source code is entered on each line,

**FIGURE 2.21**

```
     Columns . . . :  1  71              Edit           YOURLIBXX/CLOBJECT
     SEU==> _____PGMMEMBER
     FMT ** ...+... 1 ...+... 2 ...+... 3 ...+... 4 ...+... 5 ...+... 6 ...+... 7
          *************** Beginning of data ***************************************
     ''''''''
     ''''''''
     ''''''''
     ''''''''
     ''''''''
          ****************** End of data ******************************************
```

```
     F3=Exit  F4=Prompt  F5=Refresh  F9=Retrieve  F10=Cursor
     F16=Repeat find     F17=Repeat change        F24=More keys
```

the apostrophes will be replaced with line numbers. Line commands are entered in the line number area. For instance, move the cursor to the fifth line's line number area. Type **D** over any of the apostrophes and press ENTER. The member will now contain only four blank lines because the line command D deletes the line on which it is placed.

## Moving Within a Member Using SEU

SEU provides a full-screen editor, meaning characters can be edited wherever they are located on the screen. Moving the cursor with the SEU editor is similar to most word processing applications. The arrow keys control movement within the member. The up and down arrow keys move the cursor between lines, and the left and right arrow keys move the cursor between characters on the same line. Further, when the bottom or top of a screen is reached, pressing the up or down arrow key will cause the lines to scroll.

To move around the program a little faster, type the following commands at the SEU prompt and then press ENTER:

To move to the top of your program:
- Type **TOP** (or **T**).

To move to the bottom of your program:
- Type **BOT** (or **B**).

Several special keys also allow a member to be traversed more than one line at a time:

To move back a page:
- Press PAGE UP (or SHIFT-↓)

To move forward a page:
- Press PAGE DOWN (or SHIFT-↑)

To move right in the member:
- Press F20

To move left in the member:
- Press F19

To move the cursor to the SEU prompt:
- Press F10

## Entering Information

To add information to the member, move the cursor beneath the first asterisk in the Beginning of data line header and begin typing the source code or text. As shown in Figure 2.22, anything can be typed. When ENTER is pressed, however, SEU's interactive editor reads the line and, in this case, sends a message that the CL command entered is not valid (Figure 2.22). The editor knows to look for CL commands because of the member type, CLP. The error message on the bottom of the screen states that the first "command" is not a valid CL statement. Change the line to read **STRPDM**, which is the CL command to start PDM. When you press ENTER, notice that no error message is displayed because this is a valid command for a CLP member.

FIGURE 2.22

```
Columns . . . : 1 71                  Edit              YOURLIBXX/CLOBJECT
SEU==>_____ PGMMEMBER
FMT **  ...+... 1 ...+... 2 ...+... 3 ...+... 4 ...+... 5 ...+... 6 ...+... 7
        *************** Beginning of data ***********************************
0001.00 THE RAIN IN SPAIN FALLS MAINLY ON THE PLAIN
0002.00
0003.00
0004.00
        ***************** End of data ***************************************




F3=Exit  F4=Prompt  F5=Refresh  F9=Retrieve  F10=Cursor
F16=Repeat find      F17=Repeat change        F24=More keys
Command THE in library *LIBL not found.
```

## Prompting

Program code can also be entered using the prompt method. Prompting is a programmer's utility that facilitates source code entry. It can help find a command or, if the command is known, help with the syntax. To find a command, prompt (press F4) with no command specified. The prompt function will display a series of menus that allow the user to find the command. Once the command is chosen, the prompt will display a series of screens where the required and optional parameters can be entered. After the parameters have been specified and ENTER is pressed, the command will be inserted with the correct syntax at the line indicated. The prompt can be started by either pressing F4 or using an SEU line command.

To start the prompt using F4, move the cursor to the line where the command should be inserted and press F4. This will start the command search. The command can also be entered first—if you already know it—and then press F4. This will take you directly to the parameter screen.

To activate the prompt through a line command, type IP—insert with prompt—in a line's number area. This will start the command search, and after all parameters are specified, the command will be placed on that line. If the line command prompt is used, the system will continue the prompt for the next line. This will continue until a blank line is entered.

The prompt screen displayed will depend on the type of member. Different programming languages have different requirements and commands, so there are quite a number of different prompt screens.

## Editing a Member

Members can be edited by issuing several different line commands. To insert a line:

- Move the cursor to the number area of the line where the new line is to be inserted.

- Type **I**.
- Press ENTER.

If more than one line is to be inserted, type **I** followed by the number of lines to insert and press ENTER.

To delete a line:

- Type **D** in the number area of the line to be deleted.
- Press ENTER.

To delete multiple lines:

- Type **DD** in the number area of the first line to be deleted.
- Move the cursor to the last line to be deleted and type **DD** in its number area.
- Press ENTER.

The lines indicated by DD and all lines between the indicated lines will be deleted.

To copy or move a line:

- Type **C** (for copy) or **M** (for move) in the number area of the line to copy or move.
- Move the cursor to the new location for the line.
- Type **A** to copy or move the line *after* the line where the cursor is or type **B** to copy or move the line *before* the line where the cursor is.
- Press ENTER.

The line will be inserted.
To copy or move multiple lines:

- Type **CC** or **MM** in the number area of the first line to copy or move.
- Move the cursor to the last line to copy or move and type **CC** or **MM** in the number area of that line.
- Move the cursor to the new line and type **A** or **B** (for after or before).
- Press ENTER.

The copy or move multiple lines command will be executed.

## Other SEU Functions

SEU also allows the user to split the display screen and look at another member. (This function also lets users browse two other types of objects: spool files and output queues. We will discuss these in Chapter 3.)

## Browse

To browse another member:

- Press F15. This will bring up the Browse/Copy Options screen.
- Enter the member, file, and library names to be browsed at the Browse/copy member, File, and Library prompts (as an example, member BROWSEMBR in the same file and library). See Figure 2.23.
- Press ENTER.

The SEU `Edit` screen will be redisplayed, but it will contain both the original member (in the upper half of the screen) and the browsed member that was specified (in the lower half of the screen) (Figure 2.24).

The user can change the position of the "split line" (and the size of each window) by positioning the cursor and pressing F6. The split line will be moved to the line the cursor is on.

To exit the browse function:

* Move the cursor to the lower half of the screen and press F12.

**FIGURE 2.23**

```
                              Browse/Copy Options
Type choices, press Enter.
     Selection  . . . . . . . .     1            1=Member
                                                 2=Spool file
                                                 3=Output queue
     Copy all records . . . . .     N            Y=Yes, N=No
     Browse/copy member . . . .     BROWSEMBR__   Name, F4 for list
        File . . . . . . . . . .      CLOBJECT__   Name, F4 for list
           Library  . . . . . . .        YOURLIBXX_  Name, *CURLIB, *LIBL

     Browse/copy spool file . .    PGMMEMBER_    Name, F4 for list
        Job. . . . . . . . . . .     PGMMEMBER_    Name
           User . . . . . . . . .        INTROxx___   Name, F4 for list
           Job number . . . . . .          *LAST_     Number, *LAST
        Spool number . . . . . .        *LAST       Number, *LAST, *ONLY

     Display output queue . . .     QPRINT____    Name, *ALL
        Library  . . . . . . . .        *LIBL_____   Name, *CURLIB, *LIBL

F3=Exit        F4=Prompt        F5=Refresh        F12=Cancel
F13=Change session defaults    F14=Find/Change options
```

**FIGURE 2.24**

```
Columns . . . : 1 71            Edit            YOURLIBXX/CLOBJECT
SEU==> _____ PGMMEMBER
FMT ** ...+... 1 ...+... 2 ...+... 3 ...+... 4 ...+... 5 ...+... 6 ...+... 7
         *************** Beginning of data ********************************
0001.00 STRPDM
0002.00
0003.00
0004.00
         ***************** End of data ***********************************

  Columns . . . : 1 71            Browse          YOURLIBXX/CLOBJECT
SEU==> _____ BROWSEMBR
         *************** Beginning of data ********************************
0001.00 /* THIS IS THE MEMBER BEING BROWSED */
0002.00 /* THIS IS THE MEMBER BEING BROWSED */
0003.00 /* THIS IS THE MEMBER BEING BROWSED */
0004.00 /* THIS IS THE MEMBER BEING BROWSED */
         ***************** End of data ***********************************




F3=Exit  F5=Refresh  F9=Retrieve  F10=Cursor  F12=Cancel
F16=Repeat find      F17=Repeat change        F24=More keys
```

## Copying from Another Member

SEU also allows copying portions (or all) of one member into another. To copy from another member:

* Access the member to copy with the browse procedure.

- In the browse member, type **C** (or **CC**) to mark the line(s).
- In the original member, type **A** or **B** to mark the destination location.
- Press ENTER.

To copy all lines from another member:

- Type **Y** at the `Copy all records` prompt on the `Browse/Copy Options` screen.
- Press ENTER.
- In the original member, mark the "copy to" location.
- Press ENTER.

## Exiting, Saving, and Printing Members

To exit SEU:

- Press F3. This will bring up the `Exit` menu (see Figure 2.18).

The `Exit` menu offers several options.
Exit and save the file with changes:

- Type **Y** at the `Change/create member` prompt.
- Press ENTER.

Exit and not save the changes:

- Type **N** at the `Change/create member` prompt.
- Press ENTER.

Exit and print out the file:

- Type **Y** at the `Print member` prompt.
- Press ENTER.

## Compiling a Source Member

After exiting SEU, the `Work with Members Using PDM` screen will be displayed. As mentioned earlier, all source code must be translated into machine language, and compiling is the procedure to do this.

To compile a member:

- Type **14** in the option field next to the member to be compiled. (To see other available options, press F23.)
- Press ENTER.

If the member is being compiled for the first time, a message at the bottom of the screen will be displayed stating that the compile job has been submitted. If the member has been compiled before, the `Confirm Compile of Member` screen will be displayed (Figure 2.25).

To compile the member:

- Type **Y** at the `Delete existing object` prompt (to delete the program object that was the result of the previous compilation).
- Press ENTER.

A message at the bottom of the screen will be displayed stating that the compile job has been submitted.

After the job is complete, the system issues a message about the result of the compile job. To see if the program has been compiled successfully, look at the system message. At the `Work with Members Using PDM` screen, type **DSPMSG** (the display messages command) at the command line and press ENTER. This will bring up the `Work with Messages` screen (Figure 2.26). A message on this screen will state whether the job completed successfully or not.

When a member is compiled, a listing is generated. If errors existed, the listing will contain error messages and a more detailed explanation of the problems.

**FIGURE 2.25**

```
                    Confirm Compile of Member

The following object already exists for the compile operation:

  Object which exists . . . . . . . . . :  PGMMEMBER
    Library . . . . . . . . . . . . . . :    YOURLIBXX
  Object type . . . . . . . . . . . . . : *PGM

  Member to compile . . . . . . . . . . :  PGMMEMBER
  File. . . . . . . . . . . . . . . . . :  CLOBJECT
    Library . . . . . . . . . . . . . . :    YOURLIBXX

Type choice, press Enter.
Press F12=Cancel to return and not perform the compile operation.

    Delete existing object . . . . . . . N     Y=Yes, N=No




F12=Cancel
```

**FIGURE 2.26**

```
                    Work with Messages
                                               System: CHICAGO
Messages for: INTROxx

Type options below, then press Enter.
  4=Remove    5=Display details and reply

Opt  Message
                    Messages needing a reply
    (No messages available)

                    Messages not needing a reply
 _Job 040942/INTROxx/PGMMEMBER completed normally on XX/XX/XX at XX:XX:XX.




                                                        Bottom
F1=Help  F3=Exit  F5=Refresh  F6=Display system operator messages
F16=Remove messages not needing a reply  F17=Top  F24=More keys
```

## Running a Program

As covered earlier, compiling a program source code member results in a new object being created that contains machine language instructions. It is this version of the program that can be executed. Members contain only the source code version of the program, which cannot be executed by the computer. So to run the newly created program:

- Exit the Work with Members Using PDM screen.

- Access the machine-executable code by going to the Work with Objects Using PDM screen for YOURLIBXX. (Notice that a new object has been created called PGMMEMBER with a type of *PGM, Figure 2.27.)

- Type 16, the Run option, next to the object name and press ENTER.

**FIGURE 2.27**

```
                    Work with Objects Using PDM

 Library . . . . .    Position to . . . . . . .  _____
                               Position to type . . . . .  _____

 Type options, press Enter.
   2=Change        3=Copy  4=Delete 5=Display    7=Rename
   8=Display description  9=Save   10=Restore  11=Move ...

 Opt Object    Type    Attribute  Text
 __  PGMMEMBER *PGM    CLP        CL PROGRAM EXAMPLE
 __  CLOBJECT  *FILE   PF-SRC     THIS IS A SOURCE PHYSICAL FILE EXAMPLE




                                                              Bottom
 Parameters or command
 ===>_____
 F3=Exit      F4=Prompt           F5=Refresh        F6=Create
 F9=Retrieve  F10=Command entry   F23=More options  F24=More keys
```

Another way to run the program is to type the command **CALL YOURLIBXX/PGMMEMBER** at the command line of any screen and then press Enter. Using either method will result in the system submitting the newly created program to be run.

The program PGMMEMBER contains the command STRPDM; therefore, when the program is run, the STRPDM command will be executed and the AS/400 Programming Development Manager (PDM) screen will be displayed.

## Summary

PDM and SEU provide easy access for programmers to a variety of often used programming functions. PDM provides global management functions such as creating, copying, compiling, and executing. SEU, on the other hand, provides a method to change the content of members. Through SEU's full-screen editor, the programmer can enter, edit, copy, and delete individual statements within members. SEU also provides on-line syntax checking and a prompt to relieve the programmer of memorizing program language command syntax.

Since this is your first exploration of any AS/400 utility, it may be hard to fully appreciate all the user-friendly features. For instance, notice the continuity between screens: F6 is always create whether a library, an object, or a member is being created; F1 is always help; system messages always appear at the same place on the screens. This consistency makes the system much easier to use and learn. On many other systems, function keys often do not have this continuity, and certainly when accessing operating system functions and other application packages this compatibility is lost. The AS/400 has created a seamless user interface regardless of the function being executed.

## LAB EXERCISE

In this lab exercise, you will create a new library and several members that will be used throughout the rest of the chapters. If YOURLIBXX has not been created, create it now:

1.  Start PDM from any display screen. (Type **STRPDM** at any command line and press ENTER.)

2.  From the AS/400 Programming Development Manager (PDM) menu, choose option 1, Work with libraries.

3.  From the Specify Libraries to Work With screen, leave *ALL in the Library prompt and press ENTER.

4.  At the Work with Libraries Using PDM screen, press F6, the Create option.

5.  At the Create Library screen, enter **YOURLIBXX** (where your unique two-digit number is substituted for XX) at the Library prompt, your name at the Text 'description' prompt, and press ENTER. YOURLIBXX will be created by the system.

6.  When the Work with Libraries Using PDM screen is redisplayed, press F12.

Now create a new source physical file called INVSRC within YOURLIBXX. If the AS/400 Programming Development Manager (PDM) menu is not currently displayed at the workstation, type **STRPDM** at the command line and press ENTER.

1.  From the AS/400 Programming Development Manager (PDM) menu, choose option 2, Work with objects.

2.  At the Specify Objects to Work With screen, type **YOURLIBXX** in the Library prompt and press ENTER.

3.  At the Work with Objects Using PDM screen, press F6, the Create option.

4.  From the Create Commands screen, select option 126, Create Source Physical File.

5.  At the Create Source Physical File (CRTSRCPF) screen, type **INVSRC** at the File prompt and **YOURLIBXX** at the Library prompt.

6.  Press ENTER. File INVSRC will be created.

7.  When the Work with Objects Using PDM screen is redisplayed, press F12.

To create the new members:

1. From the AS/400 Programming Development Manager (PDM) menu, choose option 3, Work with members.

2. At the Specify Members to Work With screen, type **YOURLIBXX** at the Library prompt and **INVSRC** at the File prompt.

3. Press ENTER.

4. At the Work with Members Using PDM screen, press F6 to invoke the Create function.

5. At the Start Source Entry Utility (STRSEU) screen, type **ITEM** at the Source member prompt and **PF** at the Source type prompt.

6. Press ENTER.

7. From the Edit screen, press F3 to exit.

8. At the Exit screen, type **Y** at the Change/create member prompt.

9. Press ENTER. Member ITEM will be created.

10. From the Work with Members Using PDM screen, perform steps 4 through 9 to create two more source physical file members with a type of PF called BATCH and CARTON.

## REVIEW QUESTIONS

1. What are the three major storage entities on the AS/400?

2. Describe the function provided by PDM.

3. What are line commands, and how are block line commands performed?

4. How is prompting invoked?

5. What is compiling, and what is created by compiling?

6. What is the CL command to run a program?

## DISCUSSION QUESTION

1. Discuss the user-friendly features encountered so far on the AS/400. List each and explain how it either clarifies a system function(s) or makes the function(s) easier to use.

# Control Language

3

## Overview

Control Language (CL) commands are the means to execute AS/400 operating system functions. Just as DOS or OS/2 allows users to perform operating system commands on a personal computer, CL allows operating system functions such as copying files, starting system utilities, and creating libraries to be performed on the AS/400. In addition, CL allows the user to perform tasks that are needed in a multiuser computer environment (creating userids) and tasks unique to the AS/400 (creating library lists).

This chapter gives the readers an overview of the CL command structure and introduces some common CL commands. In addition, a more complicated CL program will be created, and several CL commands that are used exclusively in CL programs are introduced. How to use on-line help and prompting to find and use the correct CL commands is also covered.

After finishing this chapter, you will understand:

- The general capabilities of CL
- How CL commands are constructed
- The major CL command categories

You also will be able to:

- Use the command screens and prompts to issue CL commands from the command line
- Create, compile, and run a CL program
- Create and manipulate output queues
- Change library lists
- Display messages

## CL Commands

In keeping with the AS/400's user-friendly approach, all CL commands try to follow a common naming convention. A noncomputer example of naming conventions is the way people are named in the United States and China. In the United States, people usually have a first, a middle, and a last name, with the last name being the same as their father's. In China, the naming convention is a first and a last name, with the first name being the same as the father's. In other words, in America you would be James Tiberius Kirk, but in China you would be Kirk James.

The CL command naming convention dictates that the maximum CL command size is nine characters. Each command can be broken down into a maximum of three parts, and each part can have a maximum of three characters. The three parts are the command verb, adjective, and object (Figure 3.1).

The verb describes the work or operation that the command performs. For instance, CPY stands for copy, and CHG means change. The command adjective and object describe the object that will be operated on. For instance, SRCPF stands for a source physical file, and USRPRF represents a user profile.

**FIGURE 3.1**
**Three Parts of a Command**

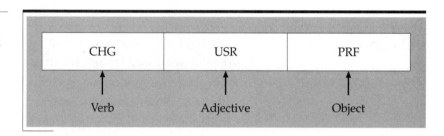

Just as Cher and Madonna are exceptions to the U.S. naming convention, there are also CL commands that are exceptions to the CL naming conventions. For instance, the CL adjective is not always necessary, nor does the adjective or object have to be three characters. Many CL commands simply have a verb and an object, with the object being represented by a single character, such as F, which stands for file.

Once the three (or fewer) character representations of the basic functions and objects are known, the correct command to use can often be guessed.

## Groups of CL Commands

There are two major ways to classify all CL commands: by verb and by the object on which they operate. For instance, there is a group of delete commands:

| | |
|---|---|
| DLTMNU | delete menu |
| DLTLIB | delete library |
| DLTUSRPRF | delete user profile |
| DLTF | delete file |

Each of these commands deletes a different object, but they all share the same verb. They all belong to the delete group.

Other common command verbs are:

STR  start

CRT   create

DSP   display

The second way CL commands can be grouped is by the objects they work against. For instance:

CPYF   copy file

SNDF   send file

RCVF   receive file

DLTF   delete file

These commands all process a file; they belong to the file group of commands. Notice that the DLTF command is included in both the file group of commands and the delete group of commands. All commands are classified by the type of processing they perform and the type of object they process.

## CL Menus

If the user cannot remember the correct CL command (and has been unsuccessful at guessing), the AS/400 provides a series of menus to help find the desired command. To display the menu of the major CL command groups, type GO MAJOR at the command line of any system screen or move the cursor to the command line of any system screen and press F4. A menu of the major CL command groups (Figure 3.2) will be displayed.

When an option from the Major Command Groups screen is selected, a submenu with a list of more command groups or a screen with a list of commands will be displayed. For instance, choosing option 2, Verb Commands, will result in a menu of verb groups such as Add Commands and Change Commands (Figure 3.3), whereas choosing option 5, File Commands, will result in a list of actual commands, in this case, commands that perform operations against files (Figure 3.4).

FIGURE 3.2

```
 MAJOR                Major Command Groups
                                                       System: CHICAGO
 Select one of the following:

        1.  Select Command by Name                     SLTCMD
        2.  Verb Commands                              VERB
        3.  Subject Commands                           SUBJECT
        4.  Object Management Commands                 CMDOBJMGT
        5.  File Commands                              CMDFILE
        6.  Save and Restore Commands                  CMDSAVRST
        7.  Work Management Commands                    CMDWRKMGT
        8.  Data Management Commands                    CMDDTAMGT
        9.  Security Commands                          CMDSEC
       10.  Print Commands                             CMDPRT
       11.  Spooling Commands                          CMDSPL
       12.  System Control Commands                    CMDSYSCTL
       13.  Program Commands                           CMDPGM
                                                              More..
 Selection or command
 ===>
 F3=Exit  F4=Prompt  F9=Retrieve  F12=Cancel  F13=User support
 F16=AS/400 Main menu
```

FIGURE 3.3

```
VERB                    Verb Commands

Select one of the following:

         1.  Add Commands                          CMDADD
         2.  Allocate Commands                     CMDALC
         3.  Answer Commands                       CMDANS
         4.  Analyze Commands                      CMDANZ
         5.  Apply Commands                        CMDAPY
         6.  Ask Commands                          CMDASK
         7.  Call Commands                         CMDCALL
         8.  Configuration Commands                CMDCFG
         9.  Change Commands                       CMDCHG
        10.  Check Commands                        CMDCHK
        11.  Close Commands                        CMDCLO
        12.  Cleanup Commands                      CMDCLNUP
        13.  Clear Commands                        CMDCLR
        14.  Compare Commands                      CMDCMP
                                                      More...

Selection or command
===>_____
F3=Exit  F4=Prompt  F9=Retrieve  F12=Cancel  F16=Major menu
```

FIGURE 3.4

```
CMDFILE                 File Commands

Select one of the following:

   Commands
         1.  Close File                            CLOF
         2.  Copy File                             CPYF
         3.  Declare File                          DCLF
         4.  Delete File                           DLTF
         5.  Delete Override                       DLTOVR
         6.  Display File Description              DSPFD
         7.  Display File Field Description        DSPFFD
         8.  Display Override                      DSPOVR
         9.  Receive File                          RCVF
        10.  Restore S/36 File                     RSTS36F
        11.  Save S/36 File                        SAVS36F
        12.  Send File                             SNDF
        13.  Send/Receive File                     SNDRCVF
                                                      More...

Selection or command
===>_____
F3=Exit  F4=Prompt  F9=Retrieve  F12=Cancel  F16=Major menu
```

Menus can also be invoked by typing the command **GO** followed by a space and the menu name. Thus, typing **GO VERB** and pressing ENTER on any system screen would do the same thing as typing **2** and pressing ENTER on the Major Command Groups screen. The question becomes how to tell the difference between menu names and CL commands. The major difference between a CL command and a command menu name is that command menu names usually begin with CMD, whereas CL commands begin with a three-character verb. To every rule, of course, there are exceptions; not all menus begin with CMD (for example, MAJOR and VERB). These exceptions can be picked out as menus, however, because they do not follow the command naming convention of verb, adjective, and object.

There are several ways to execute CL commands from the menus. The easiest is to type the option number at the command line and press ENTER. For instance, typing **4** on the `File Commands` screen (see Figure 3.4) will result in the DLTF prompt screen being displayed.

Another way to execute a CL command is to type the command at the command line and press ENTER. (Notice on these menus that to the right of each option is a CL command or a menu name.) Issuing CL commands, however, is more complicated than bringing up menus. As mentioned, CL commands can be executed by typing them at any command line and pressing ENTER. The problem with executing CL commands this way is that some commands require more data regarding the work to be done. For instance, just typing **DLTF**, for delete file, is not enough information for the operating system to work with. The name of the file to be deleted must also be supplied. These command qualifiers, or *parameters*, must be supplied in a certain order and identified by specific keywords. To execute the commands from the command line, the user must know the correct syntax and keywords.

## CL Command Syntax

Most CL commands require parameters. For instance, any command that performs an action against an object needs the object name. Sometimes there are also further qualifications regarding the type of work to be done, or there is more than one object involved in the function. For instance, CPYF—copy file—requires the name of the file to be copied and the new file name where the copy will be placed. Rather than making the user remember all the individual command keywords and parameters, the AS/400 provides a CL command *prompt* function. When the prompt function is invoked, one or more screens are displayed, listing all the possible parameters that can be supplied for the command. For each parameter, space is provided to enter a value. After you enter the values, press ENTER. This will submit the command with the correct keywords in the proper order. To invoke the prompt function for a specific CL command, type the CL command on the command line and press F4. As an example, type **CPYF** and press F4. The `Copy File (CPYF)` screen (Figure 3.5) will be displayed.

**FIGURE 3.5**

```
                        Copy File (CPYF)

 Type choices, press Enter.

 From file . . . . . . . .                Name
   Library . . . . . . . .   *LIBL       Name, *LIBL, *CURLIB
 To file . . . . . . . .                  Name, *PRINT
   Library . . . . . . . .   *LIBL       Name, *LIBL, *CURLIB
 From member . . . . . . .   *FIRST      Name, generic*, *FIRST, *ALL
 To member or label  . . .   *FIRST      Name, *FIRST, *FROMMBR
 Replace or add records  .   *NONE       *NONE, *ADD, *REPLACE
 Create file . . . . . . .   *NO         *NO, *YES
 Print format  . . . . . .   *CHAR       *CHAR, *HEX




                                                                Bottom
 F3=Exit  F4=Prompt  F5=Refresh  F10=Additional parameters  F12=Cancel
 F13=How to use this display      F24=More keys
```

Figure 3.5 shows some of the parameters that can be entered for the copy file command. For instance, there are entry areas to specify the file to be copied—the From file, library, and member—and areas that specify where the copied file should go—the To file, library, and member. As mentioned earlier, sometimes further qualification regarding the function can be specified. In the case of CPYF, the system can be instructed to create the To file during the copy function. This saves the programmer from having to execute a whole series of commands to first create and then copy the file. The F10 key provides additional parameters that can be specified for the copy file command. These include parameters to select particular records for copying (by record number or key value) or to limit the number of records to be copied.

When you are unsure of a parameter's purpose, don't forget about the on-line help. For instance, to find out more information about the From file parameter, move the cursor to the parameter field and press F1. Doing this for the From file field would result in the help window in Figure 3.6.

The help window contains several pieces of information. First, there is an explanation of what the parameter signifies. Then there is a list of all the possible values and an explanation of each value. You can enlarge the help window to take up most of the display screen by pressing F20. To retrieve further information about the command and all the parameters, press F2, Extended help. Prompting and field help are invaluable for all AS/400 users and are especially useful to new users.

After all the required parameters have been filled in, press ENTER to execute the CL command. If a required parameter has not been entered or a parameter value has been misspelled, the prompt screen will reappear with an error message and the incorrect field highlighted.

**FIGURE 3.6**

```
                            Copy File (CPYF)
Type choices, press Enter.
From file . . . . . . . . . .        Name
  Library .  ..............................................................
To file . . :            From file (FROMFILE) - Help              :
  Library . :                                                     :
From member  : Specifies the name and library of the database file or:
To member or : device file that contains the records being copied. A :
Replace or ad: database file can be a physical file or a logical file. A:
Create file  : device file can be a diskette file or a tape file.    :
Print format :                                                       :
             : The possible library values are:                      :
             :                                                        :
             : *LIBL                                                  :
             :    The library list is used to locate the database file :
             :    or device file.                                     :
             :                                              More...   :
             : F2=Extended help  F10=Move to top  F11=Search index   :
F3=Exit  F4= : F12=Cancel        F20=Enlarge       F24=More keys      :
F13=How to us:                                                        :
Parameter FRO:......................................................:
```

If there is a more complex error—for instance, a From file is specified to which the user does not have access authority—the screen from where the prompting was done will be redisplayed. At the command line for that screen will be the syntactically correct CL command, with all the previously specified parameters. There will also be an error message at the bottom of the screen stating the problem.

Rather than reentering the command and all its parameters, the user can edit the command directly on the command line or through the prompt. Pressing F4 will result in the prompt screen being displayed with all the previously specified values carried over. The command can now be changed to specify a file to which the user does have access authority. In this way, the entire command and its parameters do not have to be reentered.

## Creating Programming Objects with CL Commands

In Chapter 2, we introduced libraries, source physical files, data physical files, and members. In that chapter, we also covered how to create these objects through PDM. Rather than going through PDM, the user can directly issue CL commands that will create these objects.

To find out which command to use, the user could search the CL create commands menu. However, to save some time, the following instructions briefly explain the most frequently used create commands and the parameters that are required:

To create a library:

- Type CRTLIB.

- Press F4 to prompt for the library and type.

- Fill in the library name and library type. (Press F1 for help on the types available.)

- Press ENTER.

A message should appear at the bottom of the screen saying that the library was created.

To create a source physical file for source code members:

- Type CRTSRCPF.

- Press F4 to prompt for the library and file.

- Fill in the library name and file name.

- Press ENTER.

A message should appear at the bottom of the screen saying that the file was created in the library.

To create a source member in a source physical file:

- Type STRSEU.

- Press F4 to prompt for the library, file, member, and type.

- Fill in the library name, file name, new member name, and member type.

- Press ENTER.

- The SEU Edit screen will be displayed. Source code can be entered, or the user can exit by pressing F3.

- When the SEU Exit screen appears, a Y should always be filled in at the Create/change member prompt. (If not, then type a Y at the prompt.)

- Press ENTER.

A message should appear at the bottom of the screen saying that a member was added to the file and library specified.

To compile a program member:

There are individual commands depending on the type of program member. Here are a few of them:

- To compile a PF member, type **CRTPF**.

- To compile a CLP member, type **CRTCLPGM**.

- To compile a RPG member, type **CRTRPGPGM**.

- Press F4 to prompt for the library, file, and member to be compiled.

- Press ENTER and follow the procedure for displaying messages (see Chapter 2) to check that the compile was successful.

You may have noticed that there are more options on the various compile command prompt screens than were covered in the preceding descriptions of each function. These extra options allow the user to do things such as specify the name of the program object that will be created when the member is compiled or specify the name of the library where the program object will be contained. CL commands generally offer more options and versatility than the system interfaces and utilities. For example, during compiling with PDM, it is assumed that the program object will be in the same library as the source member, and PDM gives the program object the same name as the source member. (For instance, from the earlier example, source code member CURLEY provides the name for the program object CURLEY that is the result of compiling with PDM.) When CL commands are used, there are options to control these parameters.

Generally, as users become more involved and familiar with the AS/400, they find the easy-to-use interfaces and utilities too restrictive. Fortunately, the AS/400 has more explicit—and more complicated—tools such as CL and DDS that allow the user to exert maximum control over system functions.

## Creating an Environmentally Sound Programming Environment

Several other objects besides libraries, files, and members are commonly used by programmers. One of these is an *output queue*. Believe it or not, by utilizing output queues you can help protect the environment and save time. To understand how to use an output queue, we first have to learn about another object, called a *spool file*, and how the system uses spool files when dealing with output.

Spool files are temporary files that contain output data. (Spool stands for simultaneous peripheral operations on line.) When the system first creates output, it is written to a spool file. For instance, when a program is compiled, a compilation report is created. The compilation report is initially written to a spool file.

Next, the system must determine where the output should be sent. All output on the AS/400 is sent to a default output device. The compilation report in the spool file is the responsibility of the system processor until the default output device receives it. On the AS/400, the default output device is usually an output queue associated with a printer. Output queues are temporary storage areas on disk, and each printer has a specific disk storage area—an output queue—associated with it. The output queue holds spool files in case information is being sent faster than the printer can print it. (If the default output device was the printer, not the output queue, the system processor would not be able to send the spool file until the printer was ready. Since printers print considerably slower than processors can process, there would be a tremendous degradation in system performance.)

If the default output device is an output queue, the system processor can send the spool file to a location in secondary storage and proceed with other tasks. The printer will read the output queue when it finishes processing its current job.

Output queues do not have to be associated with a printer. There are CL commands that allow users to create output queues and change the default output device for their output. (This is where saving the world's forests comes in.) A user can create an output queue and not associate that queue with a printer but specify it as the default output device. All spool files will now be sent and stored in the new output queue. The user can then access the output queue (again, with CL commands) and decide whether to view, discard, or print the output. For instance, after reading a compilation report, a programmer may decide to discard it. If the report had been sent to an output queue not associated with a printer, it could be read at the workstation and then simply erased from storage. Automatically printing output wastes paper and clogs landfills. (It may seem like only a few sheets of paper, but over a short time and many users, it adds up to a forest's worth.)

As we mentioned, there are CL commands that enable users to create and work with output queues as well as specify an output queue as the default device for all newly created spool files. There are also commands that let users access and view the spool files at their workstations and options that let them manipulate, print, and delete spool files.

To create an output queue:

- Type **CRTOUTQ OUTQ(YOURLIBXX/MYQ)** and press ENTER.

This will create an output queue in YOURLIBXX called MYQ. To verify that the output queue has been created:

- Type **WRKOUTQ YOURLIBXX/MYQ** and press ENTER.

The screen in Figure 3.7 will be displayed. This screen is a list of all the spool files in the output queue. The output queue has no spooled files because it was just created. To place spool files on the output queue, we will define the output queue as the default output device and then generate output. Press F3 to exit this display and return to the AS/400 Main Menu.

The output queue can be defined as the default output device through the CHJOB command. Type **CHGJOB** at the command line and prompt for the parameters by pressing F4. Then press F10 for additional parameters. The screen in Figure 3.8 will be displayed.

**FIGURE 3.7**

```
                        Work with Output Queue

Queue: MYQ         Library: YOURLIBXX         Status:RLS

Type options, press Enter.
   1=Send  2=Change  3=Hold  4=Delete 5=Display 6=Release 7=Messages
   8=Attributes       9=Work with printing status


Opt  File  User  User Data  Sts  Pages  Copies  Form  Type  Pty

   (No spooled output files)




                                                           Bottom
Parameters for options 1, 2, 3 or command
===>
F3=Exit  F11=View 2  F12=Cancel  F22=Printers  F24=More keys
```

**FIGURE 3.8**

```
                        Change Job (CHGJOB)

Type choices, press Enter.

Job name . . . . . . . . . . .    *        Name, *
   User . . . . . . . . . . . .            Name
   Number . . . . . . . . . . .            000000-999999
Job priority (on JOBQ) . . . .    *SAME    0-9, *SAME
Output priority (on OUTQ). . .    5        1-9, *SAME
Print device . . . . . . . . .    PRT01    Name, *SAME, *USRPRF...
Output queue . . . . . . . . .    *DEV     Name, *SAME, *USRPRF, *DEV...
   Library . . . . . . . . . .             Name, *LIBL, *CURLIB
Run priority . . . . . . . . .    20       1-99, *SAME

                     Additional Parameters

Job queue  . . . . . . . . . .    *SAME    Name, *SAME
   Library . . . . . . . . . .             Name, *LIBL, *CURLIB
Print text . . . . . . . . . .    *BLANK
                                                        More...
F3=Exit F4=Prompt F5=Refresh F12=Cancel F13=How to use this display
F24=More keys
```

In Figure 3.8, *DEV is specified as the default output queue. *DEV is the queue associated with the printer. To change the default output queue, type **MYQ** over *DEV and **YOURLIBXX** at the Library prompt. Press **ENTER**. This will change the default destination of all the user's spooled files. To check that this is occurring, go back and recompile the CL program that was created in the last chapter. (Doing this will create a compilation report—at last, output!) Issue the **WRKOUTQ** command as before. There will be a spool file listed on the Work with Output Queue screen. You can manipulate the spool file by typing in the appropriate option number next to its name. The spool file can also be deleted or printed from this screen.

There is, however, a problem with defining the default output device with the CHGJOB command from the command line. Any changes made are only for the duration of the session. When the user signs off, the default output device reverts to the printer. The next time the user signs on, the output queue associated with the printer will be the default output queue. This makes it difficult to maintain an output queue as the default; however, there is a way around the problem. Chapter 2 covered how to create CL programs. A CL program could be written to change the output queue, and each time the user signs on, it could be run. As an example, let's create a new program that will set up the output queue as the default and initialize the programming environment in several other time-saving ways.

Create a new physical file member called INITPGM under the object and library created in the last chapter, YOURLIBXX and CLOBJECT. Use either PDM or the appropriate CL command. (Remember to specify the correct member type for CL source code.) Insert a text description for the new file as follows: **Initial student program - introxx**. For the purpose of this exercise, assume that everyone has a seven-character userid that begins with the characters *intro* and ends with a unique two-digit number. This two-digit number also matches the last two digits of the library name; for example, for the userid INTRO99, the library name is YOURLIB99.

After the member has been created, the SEU Edit screen should be displayed. The member is now ready for code to be entered.

## Programming in CL

As discussed in Chapter 2, CL commands can be entered into a file, compiled, and run just like many other programming languages. These CLPs (Control Language Programs) use special "program CL commands" to handle the unique needs of processing CL commands in a program. For instance, when some CL commands are executed, the system sends back a message on the bottom of the screen that may need to be acted on. In a program, there is no person to respond to those messages. So there is a special CL programming command that allows the program to check for system messages and perform certain logic if such a message is received. Some other commonly needed program functions are the ability to define program variables, call other programs from the CL program, send and receive variables to and from these called programs, and perform conditional logic.

CL programs allow users to perform all normal CL functions—create files, delete userids, call system utilities—and they provide a way to control the execution of other programs, even programs written in other programming languages, such as RPG and COBOL. In this way, a CLP can act as a job control manager; it can control the execution of programs based on conditions. For instance, a payroll system may consist of hundreds of programs. Based on the day of the month, different programs may be executed; for example, on the first of the month, all time cards are processed for the previous month, on the fifth, paychecks are printed, and on the seventh, all tax information is accumulated and sent to the IRS. A CLP could be written that checks what day of the month it is and executes the correct series of programs.

CLPs can also check for system error codes that are generated when called programs are executed. The CLP can then take corrective actions based on the specific codes that were returned. This can save time both for the programmer and for the customer, who relies on the successful completion of those programs.

## Creating an Initialization Program

So far the initialization program is going to define the previously created output queue, MYQ, as the destination for all spooled files. It will also define the recently created library, YOURLIBXX, as the *current library*. The current library is the first library searched whenever an object is specified without its associated library. The current library is also used as the default library whenever an object is created. The CL command CHGCURLIB can change the current library value.

Another object, called a *library list*, also affects the programming environment. A library list is a list of all the libraries that a user most commonly uses. If users want to run a particular program, they can just specify the program name. When only the program name is specified, the system goes to the library list and searches each of the libraries in the order that they are listed within the library list. (This is true except when a current library is specified. If a current library is defined, the current library is searched first, and then the remaining user libraries are searched in listed order.) So an object can be identified by its name alone if it is contained in a library that is in the library list.

For instance, say a user's library list contains the libraries shown in Figure 3.9. If program object PAYROLL was contained in library FINANCE, it could be executed by using the CL command CALL and the program name, PAYROLL. When the system saw that no library was specified, it would go to the library list and search each library in the list for a program object called PAYROLL. In this case, it would first search QSYS, then QGPL, and finally find the object in library FINANCE.

**FIGURE 3.9**
**A Library List**

Library List

QSYS
QGPL
FINANCE

Use the CL command DSPLIBL—display library list—to show the contents of the library list. Notice that it currently does not contain YOURLIBXX. To add an entry to the library list, execute the command **ADDLIBLE LIB(YOURLIBXX)**. Redisplaying the list will show that YOURLIBXX has been added. Again, the limitation with using ADDLIBLE from the command line is that the new library is deleted from the library list after the session is over. To permanently add YOURLIBXX to the library list, the ADDLIBLE command will have to be included in the initialization program.

The initialization program will also be written generically, meaning it will be written so that anyone having a userid, as described earlier, will be able to use this program. Rather than creating 99 different programs for userids INTRO01 through INTRO99, we create one program that will work for all of them.

Figure 3.10 is an example of an initialization program that will accomplish everything we have described so far. (Following a short explanation of how the program works will be a line-by-line description and definition of each command in the program.)

Notice the format for the commands. The CL command starts at the first position in each line and is followed by various keywords with values in parentheses. The general syntax for a CL command is:

```
CLcommand keyword(value) keyword(value) ......
```

This program first sets up some program variables using declare (DCL) commands. These variables will be used to store information during the program's execution. The program then reads the userid of the person who submitted the program for execution—the RTVJOBA command on line 7. On line 9, a substring function within the change variable command will strip off the last two digits of the userid; for example, if the userid was INTRO99, it would grab the 99. The program variable &NBR is set to 99 with that same command. Next, another program variable, &LIB, is set to the concatenation (see the description of the CHGVAR command that follows for a definition of concatenation) of the character string 'YOURLIB' and the variable &NBR. In our example, this would mean that &LIB is set to YOURLIB99.

**FIGURE 3.10**

```
         ...+... 1 ...+... 2 ...+... 3 ...+... 4 ...+... 5 ...+... 6 ...+
         ************ Beginning of data ******************************
0001.00 INITPGM:  PGM
0002.00
0003.00 DCL       VAR(&USER) TYPE(*CHAR) LEN(10)   /* defines      */
0004.00 DCL       VAR(&NBR)  TYPE(*CHAR) LEN(2)    /* variables    */
0005.00 DCL       VAR(&LIB)  TYPE(*CHAR) LEN(10)   /* in the program */
0006.00
0007.00 RTVJOBA   USER(&USER)                      /* retrieves the userid */
0008.00
0009.00 CHGVAR    VAR(&NBR)  VALUE(%SST(&USER 6 2))   /* changes pgm */
0010.00 CHGVAR    VAR(&LIB)  VALUE('YOURLIB' *CAT &NBR) /* variables */
0011.00
0012.00 ADDLIBLE  LIB(&LIB)     /* adds a library to the library list */
0013.00 MONMSG     MSGID(CPF0000 CPF9999)   /* monitors for messages */
0014.00
0015.00 CHGCURLIB CURLIB(&LIB)              /* sets the current library */
0016.00 CHGJOB    OUTQ(&LIB/MYQ) /* defines the default output queue */
0017.00 STRPDM                                       /* starts PDM */
0018.00           RETURN
0019.00           ENDPGM
         ************ End of data **********************************
```

The program then issues the ADDLIBLE command, using the program variable &LIB to designate YOURLIB99. Next, the program checks for two possible messages—using the MONMSG command— and allows processing to continue if either of these messages is encountered. On line 15, the program changes the current library to YOURLIB99, again using the variable &LIB to designate YOURLIB99. Finally, the program issues the change job command that sets MYQ to the default output queue and then starts PDM.

Several different CL commands are used in this program. A short description of each CL command and how it functions within the program follows. (For more detailed information, use the on-line help facility or consult the *Control Language Reference* manual.)

- **DCL**. The declare command defines program variables. All CL program variables must begin with &. The type of data (char, numeric, and so on) and its length are then defined by the TYPE and LEN keywords. In the program, a series of variables are defined that will hold the library name (&LIB), userid (&USER), and the unique two-digit number associated with each userid, for example, 99 from userid INTRO99 (&NBR).

- **RTVJOBA**. The retrieve job attributes command gets information from the system regarding the user and certain system variables, for example, the userid that submitted the job, the date the job was submitted, and the current library of the user who submitted the job for execution. In Figure 3.10, on line 7, the userid of the person who submitted the job is retrieved and placed in the variable &USER. Later in the program, the value in the variable &USER is used to determine which library should be defined as the current library and added to the library list. For example, if the value of &USER is INTRO99, YOURLIB99 should be the current library, INTRO77 then YOURLIB77, and so on.

- **CGHVAR**. The change variable command changes the value of a program variable. The VAR keyword is used to define the variable to be changed. The VALUE keyword is used to define the new value of the variable. Within the value keyword, several functions—for both numeric and string variables—are available to manipulate the variable's value:

  %**SST**. The substring function allows the programmer to identify or pick out certain characters within a character string. In the first CHGVAR command, on line 9, the substring function %SST(&USER 6 2) identifies the character string that will be used. In this case, it is the value contained in the variable &USER. In keeping with our example, the value of &USER would be the characters returned by the system from the RTVJOBA command, that is, INTRO99. The numbers following &USER specify which character to position at and how many characters to pick. In this case, the 6 and 2 tell the substring function to position itself before the sixth character and then pick the next two characters. Or in other words, pick the sixth and seventh characters of the character string. Because the substring function is within the CHGVAR command keyword VALUE, the characters specified by the substring function are the new value for the variable identified in the VAR keyword. In the program, it means that variable &NBR will be set to the sixth and seventh characters of the userid. For userid INTRO99, the value of &NBR would be changed to 99.

The second CHGVAR command, on line 10, uses a different function within the VALUE keyword:

**\*CAT**. The concatenation function attaches one character string to another. The syntax is:

```
'first character string' *CAT 'second character string'
```

On line 10 in the program, the first character string is the constant text YOURLIB. The second character string is the value contained in the variable &NBR. The result of the concatenation is a single character string. In the program, for userid INTRO99, the variable &NBR would contain the character string 99, and the result of the concatenation would be YOURLIB99. Because the concatenation function is used in the CHGVAR command, the result of the concatenation is assigned to the variable &LIB.

Through the use of the concatenation and substring functions, the program is able to isolate the unique number contained in the userid, identify the library that will be defined as the current library, and add that library to the library list. Because of this feature, the program is much more useful. It can be used by any userid that follows the INTROXX format.

At this point in the program, the library to work with has been identified. Remember that this library also contains the output queue to which all spool files will be sent.

- **ADDLIBLE**. The add library list entry command does exactly that—it adds the library specified in the command to the user's library list. As mentioned earlier, a library list is a list of all libraries that will be searched when the user requests an object and does not specify a library. The library list also defines the order of the library search. (The system defines a default library list when the userid is first created.)

  On line 12 of the program, the ADDLIBLE command adds a library to the library list of the user who submitted the program for execution. The library name to add is contained in the variable &LIB. &LIB will always contain the character string YOURLIB, concatenated to the unique two-digit number of the userid that submitted the job. &LIB's value was set in the previous CHGVAR command on line 10.

- **MONMSG**. The monitor messages command specifies actions to take based on specific messages returned by the system. Essentially the MONMSG command is telling the system that the programmer has foreseen the occurrence of this message and will handle the situation within the program. The command's syntax is:

```
MONMSG MSGID(message# message#...) EXEC(CL command)
```

The MSGID keyword allows the programmer to identify the messages to be checked, and the CL command within the EXEC keyword identifies the corrective action to take. In the EXEC clause, the programmer could send control to another section of the program (for example, GOTO program label) or start another program (for example, CALL xyz program). The subroutine or the called program would then perform some function that would, the programmer hopes, rectify the situation that caused the error message.

MONMSG also helps with another aspect of messages. Many messages require an answer. The system will not allow the program to continue executing until a message reply is given. The MONMSG command can be used to tell the system to ignore the message and allow the program to continue processing. (Ignore the message is a valid reply to a system message.) To do this, the programmer can omit the EXEC keyword. In many situations, taking no action and continuing processing is a valid course of action. When a programmer handles a message in this manner, it usually means that the situation causing the error message will not affect any future processing within the program.

For instance, one possible message that could be returned from executing the ADDLIBLE command on line 12 is `Library specified already contained in library list`. This message, when returned to the program, would suspend program execution until a reply was given. This situation (that the library is already in the library list) will not affect any future processing and, therefore, does not require any action. By specifying no EXEC parameter, the reply to the system is ignore the message and continue processing. This is the purpose of the MONMSG command on line 12.

- **CHGCURLIB**. The change current library command changes the current library to the value specified in the CURLIB keyword. The current library is used as a default by the system for object creation; that is, if no library is specified, the system assumes the user wants to create the object in the current library. On Create screens, *CURLIB is automatically filled in at the library prompt when the screen is initially displayed. If the user does not type over *CURLIB, the library defined as the current library will be used.

  In the program, line 15 sets the current library to the library name contained in variable &LIB. In the case of userid INTRO99, the current library would be defined as YOURLIB99. Since YOURLIBXX is where the user will be storing most objects, setting the *CURLIB to YOURLIBXX will save the user from having to specify YOURLIBXX when creating objects.

  Further, the current library is the first user library searched whenever an object is specified without a library. Again, since YOURLIBXX will contain most of the user's objects, the search will be performed faster since YOURLIBXX will be the first user library searched.

- **CHGJOB**. The change job command allows users to change a variety of variables regarding their programming environment. In the program on line 16, the output queue—MYQ, which resides in YOURLIB99—is defined as the destination for all spooled output. Sending output to this queue will cut down on the amount of hardcopy generated. The user will have to go into the output queue and specifically identify output to be printed. This is as opposed to the system default of having all output automatically printed.

- **STRPDM**. The start PDM command will bring up the main PDM screen each time the program executes. Since this command is in the initialization program, the PDM screen will automatically be displayed each time the programming environment is initialized.

## Testing the Initial Program

After the program has been entered, saved, and compiled (as covered in Chapter 2), it's ready to be tested. To test the program, first sign off the system. Sign on with the newly created program's name at the Program/procedure prompt and **YOURLIBXX** at the Current library prompt on the initial Sign On screen (see Figure 1.1). This tells the system to execute the program INITPGM in YOURLIBXX. Press ENTER, and the PDM menu should appear. Display the library list by typing **DSPLIBL** at the command line and pressing ENTER. The result should look similar to Figure 3.11. Note that the new library is now in the Library list and that YOURLIBXX is listed a second time with Type equal to CUR; this means it is defined as the current library.

**FIGURE 3.11**

```
                          Display Library List
                                                              System:

     Type options, press Enter.
       5=Display objects in library
     Opt  Library      Type   Text
          QSYS         SYS    System Library
          QSYS2        SYS    System Library for CPI's
          QUSRSYS      SYS    *IN USE
          QHLPSYS      SYS
          YOURLIBXX    CUR
          YOURLIBXX    USR




                                                              Bottom
     F3=Exit  F12=Cancel  F17=Top  F18=Bottom
     (C) COPYRIGHT IBM CORP. 1980, 1991.
```

## Summary

CL commands allow users to create and manipulate system resources (like output queues) and programming objects (like libraries). They also provide great control over the systems operations and allow users to customize and optimize their system environment. Though there are many CL commands, users can find particular ones by executing the GO MAJOR command and choosing options on the resulting menus and screens. Once a command is known, on-line help and the prompt facility will guide users through the process of formatting and executing the command.

CL commands can also be grouped into programs. CL programs can be written to perform system utility functions. As the chapter example showed, by using the special CL programming commands, a generic systemwide initialization utility was created. Rather than requiring users to type in a series of commands each time they signed on the systems, this utility program could be run by each user to quickly initialize his or her programming environment.

CL programs can also manage the execution of other programs. By using program variables, retrieving system information, and monitoring messages, CL programs can control the logical execution of application programs based on conditions external to the individual programs. Used this way, CL becomes a job control language.

## LAB EXERCISES

Just as the lab exercise in Chapter 2 created more source physical file members for use in later chapters, so will this exercise. However, this chapter's two new members will be created differently. The first member will be created by CL commands issued directly from the command line. The second member will be created through a CL program. This CL program will also be created in the second exercise.

EXERCISE 1  Create a new member named BATCART with a type of LF within INVSRC and YOURLIBXX as follows:

1.  Sign on to the AS/400 specifying INITPGM as the program to initially run. (This assumes INITPGM and MYQ have already been created. If not, create them at this time and run INITPGM.)

2.  Type **STRSEU** at any command line and press F4.

3.  At the appropriate prompts, fill in:

    file name as INVSRC

    library name as YOURLIBXX

    member name as BATCART

    member type as LF

4.  Press ENTER.

5.  At the SEU Edit screen, press F3 to exit.

6.  At the SEU Exit screen, type **Y** at the Create/change member prompt.

7.  Press ENTER, and member BATCART will be created.

EXERCISE 2  This exercise will create a new CL program, CRTMBR. The program will create members in YOURLIBXX and INVSRC, with the user having to specify only the new member's name and type.

1.  Perform steps 2 through 4 from the preceding exercise, this time creating a member, CRTMBR, under YOURLIBXX and INVSRC. Define its type as CLP.

2.   At the SEU Edit screen, enter the following source code into CRTMBR:

```
          ...+... 1 ...+... 2 ...+... 3 ...+... 4 ...+... 5 ...+... 6 ...+...
          **************** Beginning of data *************************
0001.00 CRTMBR: PGM        PARM(&MEM &MTYP)
0002.00
0003.00 /*************************************************************/
0004.00 /* LINE 1 IDENTIFIES THE VARIABLES FOR WHICH VALUES WILL BE */
0005.00 /* PASSED TO THE PROGRAM FROM THE USER.                     */
0006.00 /*************************************************************/
0007.00
0008.00 DCL     VAR(&MEM)   TYPE(*CHAR)  LEN(8)
0009.00 DCL     VAR(&MTYP)  TYPE(*CHAR)  LEN(3)
0010.00
0011.00 /*************************************************************/
0012.00 /* LINES 8 AND 9 DEFINE THE VARIABLES THAT WILL BE USED IN  */
0013.00 /* THE PROGRAM.                                            */
0014.00 /*************************************************************/
0015.00
0016.00 STRSEU  SRCFILE(YOURLIBXX/INVSRC) SRCMBR(&MEM) TYPE(&MTYP)
0017.00         ENDPGM
          **************** End of data *******************************
```

3.   Follow steps 5 through 7 in exercise 1 to save CRTMBR, the new CLP member.

4.   To create the new program, the member needs to be compiled. Instead of using PDM to compile, type **CRTCLPGM** (Create CL Program) at any command line and press F4.

5.   At the prompt screen, specify the program name to be created as CRTMBR in library YOURLIBXX. Specify the source member to be compiled as CRTMBR in source file INVSRC in library YOURLIBXX.

6.   Press ENTER. The member will be submitted for compiling. A message should be displayed that the program CRTMBR was created in YOURLIBXX.

7.   Work with objects within library YOURLIBXX and verify that the program object CRTMBR exists in the library.

EXERCISE 3   After the program from exercise 2 has compiled successfully, follow the steps in this exercise to create a second member under YOURLIBXX and INVSRC.

1.   From any command line, type **CALL CRTMBR ('ITBATCAR' 'LF')** to execute the CL program created in exercise 2.

2.   Follow steps 5 through 7 of exercise 1 to exit and save the new logical file member, ITBATCAR.

**REVIEW QUESTIONS**

1.   What are the three possible components of a CL command?

2.   What functions do the following three-character CL verbs represent?

     WRK

     STR

DSP

DLT

CPY

3.  What is the purpose of an initialization program?

4.  What object controls the search order the system will use to locate a program object?

5.  Explain the purpose of a current library.

6.  Explain the substring and concatenation functions.

7.  Explain the functions of the following CL commands:

CRTOUTQ

MONMSG

ADDLIBLE

CPYF

RTVJOBA

CRTCLPGM

## DISCUSSION QUESTIONS

1.  What are some of the different types of operating system functions required in a multiuser computing environment? What are the CL commands that enable AS/400 users to perform these functions?

2.  Discuss the purpose of spooling and output queues and how they contribute to saving resources and improving system performance.

3.  Give several examples of special functions required of a programming language and how CL satisfies those requirements.

4.  Discuss the advantages and disadvantages of using PDM versus CL commands to execute system functions.

# DEBUG

4

## Overview

This chapter covers the interactive DEBUG facility available on the AS/400. The pertinent CL commands (and their parameters) for creating a DEBUG environment will be discussed, as well as some general debugging techniques. Several CL commands that are valid only when in DEBUG mode will also be explained.

After finishing this chapter, you will understand:

- The concept and uses of tracing
- The concept and uses of breakpoints

You also will be able to:

- Run a program in DEBUG mode
- Activate tracing
- Set breakpoints
- Specify breakpoint display parameters

## Starting DEBUG

Unlike most of the other AS/400 utilities, the debugging functions on the AS/400 cannot be accessed through PDM. To invoke a DEBUG function, the user must remember the specific DEBUG command or, alternatively, display a menu of DEBUG commands by issuing the command GO CMDDDBG. Because of the limited access, the user may feel that the DEBUG functions are clumsy to use. Remember, it only seems clumsy in comparison to the previous functions' tie-in with the menu system. We have been using the PDM menu system as a "road map" to find the correct function. DEBUG, unfortunately, requires the user to issue the individual commands. Also, there are no screens that provide easy access to common DEBUG functions. Unlike PDM's handling of the other system functions (where the user can delete, create, compile, or edit a member from one screen), the DEBUG functions cannot be executed through function keys or option numbers. All DEBUG commands, however, are supported with prompt screens.

To start the DEBUG function (or, phrased differently, to run the program in DEBUG mode), type in **STRDBG** and press **F4**. This will bring up the Start DEBUG (STRDBG) prompt screen (Figure 4.1). On this screen, identify the program to be tested at the Library and Program prompts. Notice the other parameters available on the screen. For instance, the user can control whether a program in DEBUG mode can update production level databases. As mentioned earlier, many information system organizations group their databases into development, test, and production libraries. When a library is created on the AS/400, it can be identified as a production library. Specifying *NO in the Update production files prompt will stop updates to any file in a production library. This ensures that any erroneous processing by the untested program will not corrupt production data. Specifying *NO also means that any files updated by the program during debugging must reside in a test

**FIGURE 4.1**

```
                          Start Debug (STRDBG)

 Type choices, press Enter.

 Program . . . . . . . . . . .   *NONE_____    Name, *NONE
   Library . . . . . . . . .     _____    Name, *LIBL, *CURLIB
              + for more values  _____

                                 _____

 Default program . . . . . . .   *PGM_____    Name, *PGM, *NONE
 Maximum trace statements  . .   200_____      Number
 Trace full  . . . . . . . . .   *STOPTRC      *STOPTRC, *WRAP
 Update production files . . .   *NO_          *NO, *YES




                                                                  Bottom
 F3=Exit F4=Prompt F5=Refresh F12=Cancel F13=How to use this display
 F24=More keys
```

library. (The other parameters available on this screen will be discussed in the next section.)

After specifying the program to be tested, press ENTER. This will add the program to the *DEBUG stack*, a list of all programs currently in DEBUG mode. (You can display this list by entering DSPDBG, the display debug command, at the command line and pressing ENTER.) A maximum of ten programs can be in DEBUG mode at a time. After DEBUG has been started, programs can be added and deleted from the DEBUG stack with the ADDPGM and RMVPGM commands.

## Tracing

*Tracing* is a feature that records the order of statement execution when a program is run. Turning tracing on for a program causes a trace file to be built. When the program is run, each statement that is executed results in an entry being made to the trace file. The entry comprises the program name, the statement number executed, the recursion level, and a sequence number. (Using recursive logic is an advanced programming topic, so we ignore DEBUG's ability to track the recursion level in this discussion.) The sequence numbers indicate the order in which the statements were executed. At the end of program execution, the programmer can display the contents of the trace file and see the statement path that was followed by the program.

Being able to trace the statements executed by the program can be very useful if the program is yielding unexpected results. When the cause of a problem is unknown, the first thing a programmer tries to do is narrow down the location of the error within the program. By tracking which statements are executed, Trace eliminates the unexecuted statements as possible sources of the error.

For instance, the CL program in Figure 4.2 calculates an employee's net pay. Net pay is calculated by subtracting federal and state taxes from gross pay. Federal withholding tax is based only on the amount of gross salary, whereas the state tax rate depends on the state of residence and the gross salary. (For instance, Florida and Washington have no state income tax, but New York does.) When the program is called, the employee's gross salary and the state he or she works in must be supplied to the program.

A person living in New York and making $20,000 should have a net pay of $16,000. However, when the program is run, the result is a net salary of $19,000. To find the problem, the first step should be to set up a trace on the program. To do this, the program would have to be placed in DEBUG mode. First, issue the following command:

```
STRDBG PGM YOURLIBXX/PAY
```

Next, type **ADDTRC** and press F4 to display the Add Trace (ADDTRC) prompt screen (Figure 4.3). On this screen, a subset of program statements to be traced can be selected, or the default of *ALL—meaning trace all the program statements—can be accepted. Also on this screen, program variables can be specified. If a program variable is specified, its value will be included in the trace file. The starting values of the program variables will be the first entries into the trace file. Each time a value is changed during program execution, another entry will be made. Therefore, the trace data will consist of program variable values and statement entries intermixed.

**FIGURE 4.2**

```
 Columns . . . :   1  71              Edit                    YOURLIBXX/CLSRC
 SEU==> _____                PAY
 FMT ** ...+... 1 ...+... 2 ...+... 3 ...+... 4 ...+... 5 ...+... 6 ...+... 7
 ************** Beginning of data *****************************************
0001.00 /***********************************************************************/
0002.00 /* THIS PGM CALCS NET SALARY.                                          */
0003.00 /* LINES 10 THRU 17 CALCULATE NET SALARY AFTER FEDERAL WITHHOLDING. */
0004.00 /* LINES 18 THRU 21 CALCULATE NET SALARY AFTER STATE WITHHOLDING.    */
0005.00 /***********************************************************************/
0006.00 START:      PGM       PARM(&SAL &STATE)
0007.00            DCL       VAR(&NETSAL) TYPE(*DEC) LEN(7 2)
0008.00            DCL       VAR(&SAL) TYPE(*DEC) LEN(15 5)
0009.00            DCL       VAR(&STATE) TYPE(&CHAR) LEN(2)
0010.00            IF COND(&SAL)> 50000) +
0011.00                      THEN(CHGVAR VAR (&NETSAL) VALUE(&SAL * .65))
0012.00            IF COND(&SAL > 25000 *AND &SAL <= 50000) +
0013.00                      THEN (CHGVAR VAR (&NETSAL) VALUE(&SAL * .75))
0014.00            IF (&SAL > 15000 *AND &SAL <=25000) +
0015.00                      THEN (CHGVAR VAR(&NETSAL) VALUE(&SAL * .85))
0016.00            IF (&SAL <= 15000 +
0017.00                      THEN (CHGVAR VAR (&NETSAL) VALUE(&SAL)
0018.00            IF (&STATE = 'NY') DO
0019.00               IF (&SAL > 25000) CHGVAR &NETSAL VALUE(&NETSAL * .90)
0020.00               IF (&SAL <= 25000) CHGVAR &NETSAL VALUE(&SAL * .95)
0021.00            ENDDO
0022.00 END:       ENDPGM
 **************** End of data *********************************************




 F3=Exit  F4=Prompt  F5=Refresh   F9=Retrieve  F10=Cursor
 F16=Repeat find   F17=Repeat change        F24=More keys
```

**FIGURE 4.3**

```
                         Add Trace (ADDTRC)

Type choices, press Enter.

Statements to trace:               _
  Starting statement identifier    *ALL_____   Character value, *ALL...
  Ending statement identifier .    _____   Character value
              + for more values _
Program variables:                 _
  Program variable . . . . . . .
                                   *NONE_____
_____
_____

  Basing pointer variable . . .    _____
_____
_____
              + for more values    _____
_____
_____
              + for more values _
  Output format . . . . . . . . .  *CHAR        *CHAR, *HEX
                                                       More...
F3=Exit   F4=Prompt   F5=Refresh   F10=Additional parameters  F12=Cancel
F13=How to use this display        F24=More keys
```

The order in which Trace stores the program variables and statement entries, however, is slightly misleading. In the trace data, the line that changes the value is not the line that immediately precedes the variable value. The statement previous to the statement that immediately precedes the program value is the statement that changed the value. For instance, if the trace data consisted of three statements and then a variable value, the second statement would be the one that changed the variable, not the third. This peculiarity can sometimes lead to confusion when interpreting the trace data.

For the sample program, specify **&SAL** as a variable to be displayed and press ENTER. Reissue the **ADDTRC** command and specify **&NETSAL**. Then run the program by issuing the following command:

```
CALL PGM(YOURLIBXX/PAY) PARM(20000 NY)
```

Trace data will be generated as in Figure 4.4. The command to display trace data is DSPTRCDTA.

Looking at the trace data shows that, after the declare statements, the values for &SAL and &NETSAL are correct (0 and $20,000). The program then checks the conditions in each of the IF statements and executes correctly. (That is, only after the condition is met in line 14 does the value of net salary finally change. You can see from the trace data that it is correctly set to $17,000.)

**FIGURE 4.4**

```
                                    Display Trace Data
     Program            Instruction              Recursion Level        Sequence Number
     PAY                NETSAL                           1                            1
       Start position . . . . . . . . . . . . : 1
       Length . . . . . . . . . . . . . . . . : *DCL
       Format . . . . . . . . . . . . . . . . : *CHAR
       *Variable. . . . . . . . . . . . . . . : &NETSAL
          Type . . . . . . . . . . . . . . . . : PACKED
          Length . . . . . . . . . . . . . . . : 7 2
       '      .00'
       Start position . . . . . . . . . . . . : 1
       Length . . . . . . . . . . . . . . . . : *DCL
       Format . . . . . . . . . . . . . . . . : *CHAR
       *Variable . . . . . . . . . . . . . . . : &SAL
          Type . . . . . . . . . . . . . . . . : PACKED
          Length . . . . . . . . . . . . . . . : 15 5
       '        20000.00000'
                         Statement/
     Program             Instruction             Recursion Level        Sequence Number
     PAY                 1000                            1                            2
     PAY                 1200                            1                            3
     PAY                 1400                            1                            4
     PAY                 1600                            1                            5
       Start position . . . . . . . . . . . . : 1
       Length . . . . . . . . . . . . . . . . : *DCL
       Format . . . . . . . . . . . . . . . . : *CHAR
       *Variable . . . . . . . . . . . . . . . : &NETSAL
          Type . . . . . . . . . . . . . . . . : PACKED
          Length . . . . . . . . . . . . . . . : 7 2
     ' 17000.00'
                         Statement/
     Program             Instruction             Recursion Level        Sequence Number
     PAY                 1800                            1                            6
     PAY                 1900                            1                            7
     PAY                 2000                            1                            8
     PAY                 2100                            1                            9
       Start position . . . . . . . . . . . . : 1
       Length . . . . . . . . . . . . . . . . : *DCL
       Format . . . . . . . . . . . . . . . . : *CHAR
       *Variable . . . . . . . . . . . . . . . : &NETSAL
          Type . . . . . . . . . . . . . . . . : PACKED
          Length . . . . . . . . . . . . . . . : 7 2
     ' 19000.00'
                         Statement/
     Program             Instruction             Recursion Level        Sequence Number
     PAY                 2200                            1                           10
```

The program then encounters the IF condition that checks the value of the state variable on line 18 and again executes the appropriate statements. However, notice that statement 20 (the statement two lines before the net salary variable's value display) is incorrectly setting &NETSAL to $19,000. This would lead the tester to a closer inspection of line 20. Notice that &NETSAL is being set to 95 percent of the gross salary. This is incorrect. Net salary should equal gross salary minus *both* state and federal taxes, not just state taxes. The state tax should be calculated as 5 percent of gross salary and then subtracted from net salary. The statement in line 20 should read:

```
IF (&SAL <= 25000 CHGVAR &NETSAL VALUE(&NETSAL - (&SAL * .05))
```

A look at line 19 shows that it also should be changed.

By using DEBUG and adding trace program variables, the line that contained the incorrect calculation was quickly pinpointed. You will find tracing to be very useful in any application development effort on the AS/400.

There are a couple of other Trace features you should be aware of. We already pointed out that when trace data is displayed, the statement immediately preceding the program variable information is not the statement that changed the variable's value. The statement before the immediately preceding one is the culprit.

Another point is that the trace file has a limit of 200 statements. When the limit is reached, the AS/400 continues program execution, but no more data is entered into the trace file. The problem with this limit is that often with a complex or long program many more than 200 statements will be executed before the error is encountered. Fortunately, the action the program takes on reaching that limit can be changed. On the Start Debug prompt screen (see Figure 4.1), notice the parameter Trace full. At this prompt, the action to take when the 200-statement maximum is reached is defined. If *WRAP is specified for the Trace full parameter, the last 200 statements executed will be saved in the trace file. In other words, the latest Trace file entries will begin to replace the earlier ones. When the 201st statement is executed, the 1st statement will be dropped from the trace file. The *WRAP option is also useful for programs that are looping and then abending (abnormally ending).

The maximum number of statements recorded at any time can also be changed from the Start Debug screen (or with the CHGDBG command). Simply type in a new number over the default of 200 at the Maximum trace statements prompt. The new number, however, cannot be greater than 200.

Once the program has been executed, traced, and recoded, the old trace information is no longer needed. All trace data can be erased from the trace file with one CL command, CLRTRCDTA (clear trace data).

## Breakpoints

When a program is in DEBUG mode, programmers can define breakpoints inside a program. A *breakpoint* is a point in a program where program execution is suspended and control is returned to the programmer at the workstation. When a breakpoint is reached, the Display Breakpoint screen is shown.

For a breakpoint to be set, DEBUG must be active. The command ADDBKP allows the user to specify a condition, statement number, or statement name within a program at which the breakpoint is to occur. Figure 4.5 shows the Add Breakpoint screen with the associated parameter prompts to do this. If a particular statement is identified as the breakpoint, it will be the first statement executed after the program is reactivated. This, of course, implies that program execution stops at the statement number before the one identified as the breakpoint. In other words, if statement number 100 is identified as the breakpoint (entering '/100' at the Statement identifier prompt in Figure 4.5), all statements up to and including 99.99 will be executed. When the program is reactivated, statement 100 will be the first statement executed.

The ADDBKP command also lets the user specify program variables to be displayed when the breakpoint is reached. The program variable values will be displayed on the Display Breakpoint screen, which is automatically shown when the breakpoint is reached.

**FIGURE 4.5**

```
                      Add Breakpoint (ADDBKP)

Type choices, press Enter.

Statement identifier . . . . . . _____        Character value

                 + for more values _____
Program variables:
   Program variable . . . . . . . *NONE_____
_____

_____
   Basing pointer variable . .    _____
_____

_____
                 + for more values _
Output format . . . . . . . . . . *CHAR      *CHAR, *HEX
Program . . . . . . . . . . . . . *DFTPGM___  Name, *DFTPGM
                                                     Bottom
F3=Exit F4=Prompt F5=Refresh F10=Additional parameters F12=Cancel
F13=How to use this display F24=More keys
```

The data on the Display Breakpoint screen is similar to the information on the Display Trace Data screen. The difference is that the breakpoint values displayed are the current values for the program variables. Trace data is a picture of what the values were. A breakpoint stops program execution and displays the current values of the breakpoint variables.

The user has several options at a breakpoint: The program can be restarted by pressing ENTER; program execution can be ended (not suspended) by pressing F3; or the user can press F10 and go into command entry mode. Pressing F10 results in a screen where the user can execute CL commands. A number of breakpoint-specific CL commands provide unique functions that can be executed only during a breakpoint.

For instance, if the debugger forgot to specify a breakpoint variable in the ADDBKP command, there's no need to worry. Any program variable's value can also be displayed at a breakpoint by using the DSPPGMVAR (display program variable) command.

From the `Display Breakpoint` screen, press F10 to go into command entry mode. Then enter the **DSPPGMVAR** command with the variable name. The program variable definition and value will be displayed.

Another special CL command that can be executed during a breakpoint is the CHGPGMVAR (change program variable) command. This command allows the user to change a variable value at a breakpoint. As with the DSPPGMVAR command, the program and variable names must be specified. After a program variable has been viewed and changed, the program can be reactivated. First, exit from command entry mode by pressing F3. Then press ENTER at the `Display Breakpoint` screen. The program will restart execution at the breakpoint statement.

An interesting use of breakpoints and the CHGPGMVAR command is in testing partially written programs. For instance, if two-thirds of a program had been written (the first third and the last third) and the programmer wanted to see if those portions were working correctly, processing of the middle third could be simulated through the use of a breakpoint and the CHGPGMVAR command. By placing a breakpoint at the end of the first third of the program and then issuing CHGPGMVAR commands to set the program variable values to appear as if processing of the middle third had occurred, a programmer could test the final third.

For instance, say the first third calculates an employee's pay, the middle third updates files with the pay information and retrieves the employee's address, and the final third prints out a check and an addressed envelope. At the end of the pay calculation, a breakpoint would be inserted. When the breakpoint is reached, the programmer would make sure that the pay has been calculated correctly. If so, the program's address variable could be set to some value, and the program would be allowed to continue executing. The paycheck and envelope would be printed and checked to see if they are correct. In this way, a programmer doesn't have to wait till the program is completely written or the data files are established in order to start testing. By stopping execution and manipulating the data, breakpoints and the CHGPGMVAR command can also test programs that call other programs or use, as of yet, unwritten subroutines.

## Summary

The AS/400 provides several debugging tools for programmers. These utilities include:

- A Trace feature that allows programmers to record and view the logic path followed by a program. It also provides information regarding the definition and value of program variables.
- A Breakpoint function that stops program execution and displays the current values of program variables.

Several special DEBUG CL commands also allow the programmer to monitor, maintain, and manipulate the DEBUG environment. These commands allow the user to:

- Add and delete programs from the DEBUG stack
- Display the DEBUG stack
- Clear out the trace file
- Display and change program variables during breakpoints

Together, these functions provide an effective environment to test programs and identify program problems.

**LAB EXERCISE**

This lab exercise will set up breakpoints within a program and then perform some of the CL commands specific to breakpoints and DEBUG. The program to be used is CRTMBR, which was created in the lab exercise to Chapter 3.

To define a breakpoint:

1. Start DEBUG by typing **STRDBG** at any command line and pressing F4.

2. Specify:
   a. **CRTMBR** at the `Program` prompt. (This will add CRTMBR to the DEBUG stack.)
   b. **CRTMBR** at the `Default program` prompt. (This will save you from having to specify the program name every time a CL DEBUG command is executed.)
   c. **\*YES** at the `Update production files` prompt. (This will allow CRTMBR to create a new member in INVSRC, a production file, while in DEBUG mode.)

3. Press ENTER.

4. To confirm that CRTMBR has been added to the DEBUG stack, type **DSPDBG** at the command line and press ENTER. Look for CRTMBR at the end of the list of programs. After confirming that the program is on the list, press ENTER to return to the command line.

5. At the command line, type **ADDBKP** and press F4.

6. At the `Add Breakpoint` screen, enter **'/7'** at the `Statement identifier` prompt and **'&MEM'** at the `Program variable` prompt. Press ENTER.

To change program variable values at a breakpoint:

1. Execute the create member program by typing **CALL CRTMBR ('NEW' 'PF')** at any command line and pressing ENTER.

2. Notice at the `Display Breakpoint` screen that the current value of the member name variable is 'NEW', exactly as was specified in the CALL command.

3. Press F10 to go into command entry mode.

4. Display the value of the member type field by typing the display program variable command as follows: **DSPPGMVAR '&MTYP'**. Press ENTER.

5. Notice that the member type field also contains the correct value, PF. Press ENTER to return to command entry mode.

6. Change the two program variable values by issuing the following change program variable commands: **CHGPGMVAR '&MEM' SLICK** and **CHGPGMVAR '&MTYP' CLP**.

7. Press F3 to exit command entry mode and return to the Display Breakpoint screen.

8. Continue executing the create member program by pressing ENTER.

9. When the program executes the STRSEU command, the SEU Edit screen will be displayed. Notice that the member being edited is SLICK. The CHGPGMVAR commands changed the file name and type values that were specified in the initial call of the program to SLICK and CLP.

10. Exit and save member SLICK.

11. To remove CRTMBR from the DEBUG stack and end DEBUG, type **ENDDBG** and press ENTER.

---

**REVIEW QUESTIONS**

1. What information is contained in trace data?
2. What is the DEBUG stack?
3. Explain tracing.
4. What is the difference between a program variable value displayed through Trace and one displayed through breakpoints?
5. Is the breakpoint statement executed before program execution is suspended or after execution is resumed?
6. How is production level data safeguarded by DEBUG?
7. What is the purpose of the Trace full parameter?

---

**DISCUSSION QUESTIONS**

1. Discuss the uses of tracing and breakpoints in finding program errors and testing.
2. Discuss some of the limits and peculiarities of the AS/400 Trace function.
3. Describe several functions that can be executed at a breakpoint.

# Screen Design Aid

# 5

## Overview

In this chapter, we explore Screen Design Aid (SDA), a utility that enables programmers to quickly and easily create screens and menus. As mentioned earlier, DDS can be used to define both files and screens. SDA allows the user to define screens in an interactive hands-on manner. By using SDA, the programmer does not have to know DDS commands, parameter keywords, or their syntax. The user first describes and constructs the screen with SDA. SDA then generates and compiles the DDS, thereby creating a display file. The display file contains the machine-understandable definition of the screen.

SDA also provides several editing functions and commands to easily define and manipulate fields on the screen. For instance, SDA is tightly coupled with the AS/400 database. Fields from existing files can be used to define screen fields. If a field is chosen from a file, it is not necessary to respecify the field characteristics. The field's database definition is used to create the display field.

A final advantage of SDA is that it allows screens to be displayed and tested throughout the development process. User-written programs do not have to be created to do this. Instead, SDA provides a test utility that works with all SDA-defined screens.

After finishing this chapter, you will understand:

- The relationship between display files and DDS source members
- The advantages of using SDA over DDS to define and test screens
- The relationship between SDA and the AS/400 database management system

You also will be able to:

- Define a screen to be used in an interactive program
- Save, compile, and reedit the display definition source member
- Display the screen with test data and check the screen's input buffer
- Create a menu

## Starting SDA

SDA, like most AS/400 utilities, can be invoked through a CL command or a series of user-friendly menus. To skip over the non-SDA menus, type **STRSDA** and press ENTER. The AS/400 Screen Design Aid (SDA) screen will appear (Figure 5.1). To create a screen, select option 1. This will result in the Design Screens screen (Figure 5.2). On this display, the user specifies the member that will contain the screen definition source code. Type the member name along with its library and file names and press ENTER. The Work with Display Records screen will be displayed (Figure 5.3).

FIGURE 5.1

```
                    AS/400 Screen Design Aid (SDA)

Select one of the following:

     1. Design screens
     2. Design menus
     3. Test display files












Selection or command
===>_____

F1=Help    F3=Exit    F4=Prompt    F9=Retrieve    F12=Cancel
```

**FIGURE 5.2**

```
                              Design Screens
 Type choices, press Enter.

     Source file  . . . . . . .    INVSRC____   Name, F4 for list

        Library. . . . . . . .     YOURLIBXX_   Name, *LIBL, *CURLIB

     Member . . . . . . . . .      INVDSPF___   Name, F4 for list












     F3=Exit        F4=Prompt           F12=Cancel
```

**FIGURE 5.3**

```
                         Work with Display Records
 File. . . . . . . :    INVSRC          Member . . . . . . : INVDSPF

    Library . . . . :    YOURLIBXX    Source type. . . . : DSPF

 Type options, press Enter.
    1=Add               2=Edit comments        3=Copy            4=Delete
    7=Rename            8=Select keywords    12=Design image

 Opt   Order   Record     Type  Related Subfile  Date   DDS Error

 1_            ITEM_____
    (No records in file)






                                                                  Bottom
    F3=Exit                    F12=Cancel     F14=File-level keywords
    F15=File-level comments    F17=Subset     F24=More keys
```

Each screen definition is stored in a *display record*, which will contain the DDS source code that SDA generates based on your screen design. To create a new display record, type **1** in the Opt column and specify a record name in the Record column. Pressing ENTER will bring up the Add New Record screen (Figure 5.4). The name of the record and its type, RECORD, will be displayed. Press ENTER to go to the Work screen (Figure 5.5).

**FIGURE 5.4**

```
                        Add New Record
 File . . . . . . :  INVSRC          Member . . . . . . :  INVDSPF
   Library  . . . :   YOURLIBXX      Source type. . . . :  DSPF
 Type choices, press Enter.

   New record . . . . . . . . . .   ITEM_____   Name

   Type . . . . . . . . . . . . .   RECORD        RECORD,  USRDFN
                                                  SFL,     SFLMSG
                                                  WINDOW,  WDWSFL




 F3=Exit      F5=Refresh      F12=Cancel
```

**FIGURE 5.5**

```




                                    .                    ~




    *                    ~




 Work screen for record ITEM: Press Help for function keys.
```

## Defining a Screen

SDA allows the programmer to define and position three types of display fields: constant text fields, system variable fields, and data fields.

## Defining Constant Text Fields

To specify a constant text field, simply type the text at the location on the screen where it should appear. If the constant text contains more than one word, enclosing it in single quotes is often a good idea. If the text is not enclosed in quotes, SDA will treat each word as a field. For a function like highlighting or underlining to be performed on all the text, each word would have to be individually highlighted or underlined. But if the text is enclosed in quotes, all the text can be operated on at once.

For our example, we first want to assign a screen name. A screen name is an example of a screen text constant. Move the cursor to the fourth line on the screen, type **'ITEM UPDATE SCREEN'** and press **ENTER**. The single quotes will disappear, and the screen name text will remain.

## Defining System Variable Fields

To define a system variable as an output field, the appropriate system variable code has to be entered on the screen. For this screen, specify that two system variable fields—time and date—will appear on the second line of the screen. To do this, move the cursor to line 2, column 1, and type *TIME. This system variable code tells the system to display the time at that position on the screen. On the far right-hand side of the line, specify the date by typing *DATE at column 63.

Counting off 62 spaces to find column 63 is rather tedious, isn't it? SDA provides a *ruler* to clearly identify line and column numbers. Move the cursor to line 3 and press **F14** to display the ruler. The ruler numbers each row and column on the Work screen. The numbers will not appear on the final screen and can be typed over. The ruler makes it much easier to find column 63. To turn the ruler off, press **F14** a second time. **F14** acts as a toggle switch, turning the ruler alternately on and off when it is pressed.

Some other system variables that can be specified include:

*USER          supplies the userid

*SYSNAME       supplies the name of the system

## Defining Data Fields

Fields that will display or accept data can be defined two different ways. If the data element already exists in a database, its DDS definition can define the screen field. If the field is not in a database, it is a user-defined data field.

To add database fields to the screen, press **F10** on the Work screen. The Select Database Files screen will be displayed (Figure 5.6). From this screen, the user can select fields from a single file or multiple files. Simply specify the file, library, and record format names in the appropriate columns. There are also four options for each file. Option 1 allows the user to pick selected fields from the file. Options 2, 3, and 4 select all the fields from the file and designate whether the fields will be used for, respectively, input only, output only, or both input and output.

Choosing option 1 will result in the Select Database Fields screen being displayed with all the fields for the database listed (Figure 5.7). Each field's length, type, and header text will also be displayed. On this screen, fields can be selected by designating them as input, output, or both. Once the options have been typed (as in Figure 5.7), press **ENTER** twice and the Work screen will reappear. Notice on the Work screen that the selected fields appear at the bottom of the screen (Figure 5.8). They are there to remind the user which database fields have been selected for placement on the screen.

**FIGURE 5.6**

```
                      Select Database Files
Type options and names, press Enter.
  1=Display database field list
  2=Select all fields for input (I)
  3=Select all fields for output (O)
  4=Select all fields for both (B) input and output

Option  Database File  Library      Record
  1     STOCKQTY__     YOURLIBXX_   STKFMT____
  _     _____     _____    _____
  _     _____     _____    _____
  _     _____     _____    _____




F3=Exit      F4=Prompt      F12=Cancel
```

**FIGURE 5.7**

```
                     Select Database Fields
Record . . . . : STKFMT

Type information, press Enter.
  Number of fields to roll. . . . . . . . . . . . .     8
  Name of field to search for . . . . . . . . . . . _____

Type options, press Enter.
  1=Display extended field description
  2=Select for input (I), 3=select for output (O), 4=Select for both (B)

Option   Field    Length     Type    Column Heading
  4      ITMNUM       6        A      ITEM NUMBER
  4      ITMNME      15        A      ITEM NAME
  _      QTYNST     6,0        P      QUANTITY IN STOCK


                                                        Bottom
F3=Exit   F12=Cancel
```

To place a field on the screen, *work screen symbols* need to be used. An example of a work screen symbol is an ampersand followed by one of the numbers that precedes a database field name at the bottom of the Work screen and the letter L (&1L). The ampersand designates the starting location of the field, and the L says that the header text is to appear to the left of the field followed by a colon. Two blank spaces will separate the colon from the start of the screen field. Type **&1L** at row 7, column 25, and type **&2L** at row 10, column 25.

After entering the work screen symbols, press ENTER. The work screen symbols will be replaced by characters that depict the length of the fields and their type. For instance, the character I says the

**FIGURE 5.8**

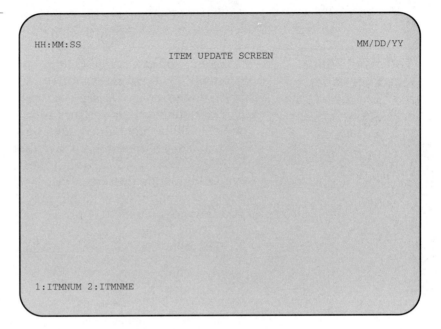

```
HH:MM:SS                                                    MM/DD/YY
                        ITEM UPDATE SCREEN




1:ITMNUM 2:ITMNME
```

field is for character input only; O, for character output only; and so on. Further, the headers will appear where dictated by the work screen symbol.

## Creating User-Defined Fields

To add a user-defined field, type + at the position before where the field is to begin on the screen. The plus sign is an *attribute character* that designates the field as user defined.

The next character entered after the plus sign defines the field type. Some codes that can be entered and their definition are:

3    numeric input only

6    numeric output only

9.    numeric input and output

I    character input only

O    character output only

B    character input and output

The next characters after the character type define the length of the field and, optionally for numeric fields, how many decimal places will be needed. The length can be denoted by either repeating the field type character the number of times of the length—+IIIIIIII for a nine-character input-only field—or using a shorthand notation—+I(9). The same holds for numeric fields: +3333333.33 and +3(7,2) both describe a nine-digit numeric input-only field with two decimal places.

For our example, define a message area on the last line of the screen. At column 5, type **+O(70)** and press **ENTER**. SDA will display the new field as dictated by the plus sign and the length parameters. SDA will also assign the field a name of FLDxxx, where xxx begins with 001 and progresses by one for each user-defined field. Thus, the first user-defined field would be FLD001, the next would be FLD002, and so on. For the message field, define a constant text header to the left of it. Start in the first column and type **MSG:**.

## Defining Field Characteristics

As mentioned, each screen field can have attribute characters associated with it. *Attribute characters* define the field and how it will appear on the screen. *Display characters*, which are a type of attribute character, define characteristics such as the field color or whether the field will be highlighted, underlined, or blinking. These attributes can be specified in the space that immediately precedes the field, the *attribute field*. To find the attribute field, press F20. F20 reverse highlights the screen field, including any preceding blank spaces. Through reverse highlighting, the field is clearly defined, and the space immediately preceding the field (the attribute field) can be easily located.

The following codes can be specified in the attribute field:

B    blink

H    highlight

R    reverse image

U    underline

The following color codes can also be specified:

CB   blue

CG   green

CP   pink

CR   red

CT   turquoise

CW   white

CY   yellow

For the screen name, we will specify an *action attribute*. Type **AC** starting in the attribute field of the screen header. AC is the code to center a field. The attribute characters will appear to overtype the first letter of the screen name. Press ENTER. The first character of the screen name will be restored, and the screen name will be centered on the line.

Another way to specify a field's attributes as well as define editing and auditing functions is to type * in a field's attribute field and press ENTER. This will invoke a series of prompt screens that allow the user to select a field's attributes or editing functions. The prompt screens free the programmer from having to remember all the attribute characters and symbols.

The first screen to appear, after the user places an asterisk in the attribute field and presses ENTER, is the Select Field Keywords screen. This screen's option list changes based on the type of field being defined. For instance, if the data field was defined as output only, the Input keywords option would not be displayed. Similarly, if the field was defined as character, the Editing keywords option would not be displayed because editing keywords are for numeric fields only. The screen displayed in Figure 5.9 shows all the possible options.

```
                    Select Field Keywords

  Field . . . . . : FLD008        Usage . . : B
  Length. . . . . : 7,2           Row . . . : 15  Column . . : 16

  Type choices, press Enter.
                                  Y=Yes For Field Type

    Display attributes . . . . .    -   All except Hidden
    Colors . . . . . . . . . . .    -   All except Hidden
    Keying options . . . . . . .    -   Input or Both
    Validity check . . . . . . .    -   Input or Both, not float
    Input keywords . . . . . . .    -   Input or Both
    General keywords . . . . . .    -   All types
    Editing keywords . . . . . .    -   Numeric Output or Both
    Database reference . . . . .    -   Hidden, Input, Output, Both
    Error messages . . . . . . .    -   Input, Output, Both
    Message ID (MSGID) . . . . .    -   Output or Both

    TEXT keyword . . . . . . . .    _____

  F3=Exit     F12=Cancel
```

Choosing an option from the `Select Field Keywords` screen will result in a screen that displays a list of potential attributes and keywords. From these screens, the user can select any attribute he or she likes. For instance, typing **Y** at the `Display attributes` prompt will result in the `Select Display Attributes` screen being displayed (Figure 5.10). From this screen, the field can be underlined, highlighted, and so on. Notice that in the upper left-hand corner there is a space for the name of the field being defined. Other areas show the field's location on the screen, length, and usage (input, output, and so on).

```
                    Select Display Attributes

  Field . . . . . : FLD001        Usage . . : O
  Length . . . . . : 70           Row . . . : 24  Column . . : 6

  Type choices, press Enter.
                                  Keyword   Y=Yes   Indicators/+
  Field conditioning . . . . . . .            _      __ __ __
  Display attributes:             DSPATR
    High intensity . . . . . . . .  HI        _      __ __ __
    Reverse image . . . . . . . .   RI        _      __ __ __
    Column separators . . . . . .   CS        _      __ __ __
    Blink . . . . . . . . . . . .   BL        _      __ __ __
    Nondisplay . . . . . . . . .    ND        _      __ __ __
    Underline . . . . . . . . . .   UL        _      __ __ __
    Position cursor . . . . . . .   PC        _      __ __ __

  F3=Exit     F12=Cancel
```

Selecting the Colors option will bring up the Select Colors screen (Figure 5.11). This screen allows the user to define the color of all characters and numbers that will appear in the field. In addition to allowing the user to define one color for a field, this screen allows a field's color to be controlled by the program that will be using it. This is done by associating an indicator with a color. If the specified indicator is set on, the field will be displayed in the indicator's associated color. The program logic can turn indicators on and off based on conditions.

For instance, it is customary to display serious error messages in red (the better with which to catch the user's eye!). Typing 30 in the indicator column on the red row would associate indicator 30 with red. Each time the program is about to display a message, it could check the message severity. If the message is concerned with a serious error, the program would turn indicator 30 on, thereby turning the error message field red. Through the use of indicators, an entire error message color scheme could be set up based on the severity of the message. (For example, green messages would mean everything is fine, informational messages would be in white, yellow would be used for minor errors, pink would signal more serious problems, and red would mean, "Step away from the terminal and keep your hands away from the keyboard.")

Choosing the other Select Field Keywords options will allow the user to define the following attributes and keywords:

- Keying options. For input fields, allows the user to define the fields as mandatory fill or entry. Gives the user the ability to set the justification of all input values and define the fill characters (blanks or zeros). These options correspond to the DDS keyword, CHECK.

- Validity check. Allows input values to be compared to a single value, a list of values, or a range of values. This allows the

**FIGURE 5.11**

```
                         Select Colors
     Field . . . . :    FLD001      Usage . . : O
     Length . . . :    70          Row . . . : 24    Column . . . : 6

     Type choices, press Enter.

                                        Keyword Order Indicators/+
                                                  (1-7)
     Colors:                            COLOR
        Blue . . . . . . . . . . . . . .    BLU      _      __ __ __
        Green . . . . . . . . . . . . .     GRN      _      __ __ __
        Pink . . . . . . . . . . . . . .    PNK      _      __ __ __
        Red . . . . . . . . . . . . . .     RED      _      __ __ __
        Turquoise . . . . . . . . . . .     TRQ      _      __ __ __
        White . . . . . . . . . . . . .     WHT      _      __ __ __
        Yellow . . . . . . . . . . . . .    YLW      _      __ __ __




     F3=Exit  F12=Cancel
```

user to define the values to be used in the DDS keywords, RANGE, COMP, and VALUES.

- `Input keywords`. Lets the programmer set up response indicators. These will be turned on if the input field is changed, blanks are entered, or DUP is pressed. The program can check the value of the response indicators to determine if any of these conditions has occurred.

- `General keywords`. Allows the user to set up another name that the field can be referenced by or define a default value that will be shown in the field when the screen is displayed. The default value displayed can be typed over by the user. This corresponds to the functions of the ALIAS, DFT, and DFTVAL DDS keywords.

- `Editing keywords`. Lets the user specify the EDTCDE and EDTWRD parameters for the screen field. These parameters designate numeric formatting functions like suppressing leading zeros; the type of thousands separator to be used; whether the negative sign should be displayed, and if so, where it should be displayed, before or after the number.

- `Database reference`. Allows the user to assign an already defined database field's definition to the current field. This option also allows some overriding of the database definition.

- `Error messages` and `Message ID (MSGID)`. Allow the user to define error messages, associate message identifiers with the message, and assign indicators for program control.

Before leaving the `Work` screen, add another text constant field that identifies the F3 key as the exit key. The `Work` screen should look like Figure 5.12.

**FIGURE 5.12**

```
HH:MM:SS                                                    MM/DD/YY

                        ITEM UPDATE SCREEN

        ITEM NUMBER: BBBBBB

          ITEM NAME: BBBBBBBBBBBBBBBB










          PRESS F3 TO EXIT THIS DISPLAY


MSG: OOOOOOOOOOOOOOOOOOOOOOOOOOOOOOOOOOOOOOOOOOOOOOOOOOOOOOOOOOOOOO
```

## Saving and Compiling

To generate and save the DDS for the screen, press F3. The Exit SDA Work Screen will be shown (Figure 5.13). For our example, save all the changes by selecting option 1. This will display the Work with Display Records screen (Figure 5.14). Notice there is now a record entry for ITEM, which we just defined. Pressing F3 again will result in the Save DDS - Create Display File screen being displayed (Figure 5.15). The library, file, and members specified earlier as the destination for the DDS will be filled in on the screen. To save the DDS code, type Y at the Save DDS source prompt.

**FIGURE 5.13**

```
                        Exit SDA Work Screen

    Select one of the following:

            1. Save work since last Enter and exit work screen
            2. Exit without saving any work done on the work screen
            3. Resume work screen session












    Selection
      _
    F12=Cancel
```

**FIGURE 5.14**

```
                    Work with Display Records

    File . . . . . . . : INVSRC          Member . . . . . . : INVDSPF
       Library  . . . . :   YOURLIBXX     Source type  . . . : DSPF

    Type options, press Enter.
       1=Add      2=Edit comments     3=Copy         4=Delete
       7=Rename   8=Select keywords   12=Design image

    Opt  Order   Record    Type    Related Subfile  Date      DDS Error
     __   _____
     __     _10   ITEM      RECORD                   01/15/93



                                                               Bottom
    F3=Exit                     F12=Cancel    F14=File-level keywords
    F15=File-level comments  F17=Subset    F24=More keys
    Record ITEM added to member INVDSPF.
```

**FIGURE 5.15**

```
             Save DDS - Create Display File

 Type choices, press Enter.

     Save DDS source . . . . . . . .  Y          Y=Yes
        Source file . . . . . . . . .  INVSRC____  F4 for list
          Library . . . . . . . . . .  YOURLIBXX_  Name, *LIBL ...
        Member . . . . . . . . . . .   INVDSPF___  F4 for list
        Text . . . . . . . . . . . .              _____

     _____
     Create display file . . . . . . .  Y          Y=Yes
        Prompt for parameters . . . . .  _          Y=Yes
        Display file. . . . . . . . . .  ITEMDSPF__  F4 for list
          Library . . . . . . . . . .   YOURLIBXX_  Name, *CURLIB
        Replace existing file . . . . .  _          Y=Yes

     Submit create job in batch  . . .  Y          Y=Yes

     Specify additional
        save or create options. . . . .  _          Y=Yes

 F3=Exit        F4=Prompt        F12=Cancel
```

To compile the DDS source code and create the display file, make sure there is a Y at the Create display file and Submit create job in batch prompts. The Library and Display file names can also be specified. Press ENTER. The DDS will be compiled, and the display screen created as specified.

## Testing Screens

SDA provides the user with the capability to see screens as they will be displayed at the user's workstation. It also lets the tester specify data for output, manipulate indicators, and see the effect on the screen appearance. For input fields, the tester can enter data in the display fields, test any defined validity checks, and inspect the input buffer that is passed back to the application program.

To go into test mode, choose option 3, Test display files, from the AS/400 Screen Design Aid (SDA) screen (see Figure 5.1). This will bring up the Test Display File screen, where the library, file, and record to be tested are specified (Figure 5.16). Once the information has been entered, press ENTER.

The test facility cycles through three screens (with the third screen providing an optional screen to view the input buffer). These three screens are the Set Test Output Data screen, the user's screen that was defined through SDA, and the Display Test Input Data screen. The user progresses through the screens by pressing ENTER.

For instance, after the display to be tested has been specified, the Set Test Output Data screen is displayed (Figure 5.17). On this screen, the tester can type in values for any field that has been defined for output and turn any display attribute indicators on or off. After specifying the output information, pressing ENTER will result in the user-defined screen being displayed with the values specified and the attributes dictated by the indicators. In Figure 5.18, the screen has no values displayed because

**FIGURE 5.16**

```
                        Test Display File

  Type choices, press Enter.
  Display file. . . . . . . . .      ITEMDSPF__  Name, F4 for list
     Library . . . . . . . . . .     YOURLIBXX_  Name,
                                                 *LIBL ...

  Record to be tested . . . . . .    ITEM_____  Name,
                                                 F4 for list
  Additional records to display .    _____  Name
                                     _____
                                     _____










  F3=Exit        F4=Prompt        F12=Cancel
```

none were specified on the Set Test Output Data screen. The user-defined screen in Figure 5.18 can, however, accept input. Typing in values, as seen in Figure 5.19, and pressing ENTER, will bring up the Display Test Input Data screen (Figure 5.20). This screen displays each input field (notice that FLD001 is not listed—it was defined as output only) and the value contained in that field. To see the input buffer layout and the contents that the application program would receive, press F14.

**FIGURE 5.17**

```
                          Set Test Output Data

    Record . . . : ITEM

    Type indicators and output field values, press Enter.

    Field      Value
    ITMNUM     BBBBBB:_____
    ITMNME     BBBBBBBBBBBBBBBB:_____
    FLD001     OOOOOOOOOOOOOOOOOOOOOOOOOOOOOOOOOOOOOOOOOOOOOOOOOOOOOO








                                                          Bottom
    F3=Exit    F12=Cancel
```

FIGURE 5.18

```
13:59:48                                                    1/15/95

                         ITEM UPDATE SCREEN

          ITEM NUMBER: BBBBBB

           ITEM NAME : BBBBBBBBBBBBBBB




              PRESS F3 TO EXIT THIS DISPLAY


MSG: OOOOOOOOOOOOOOOOOOOOOOOOOOOOOOOOOOOOOOOOOOOOOOOOOOOOOOOOO
```

Pressing ENTER again would redisplay the Set Test Output Data screen, (Figure 5.21.) Figure 5.22 simulates the message and what the screen would look like if whole milk was already in the database.

FIGURE 5.19

```
13:59:48                                                    1/15/95
                         ITEM UPDATE SCREEN

          ITEM NUMBER: 111111

           ITEM NAME : WHOLE MILK




              PRESS F3 TO EXIT THIS DISPLAY


MSG: OOOOOOOOOOOOOOOOOOOOOOOOOOOOOOOOOOOOOOOOOOOOOOOOOOOOOOOOO
```

**FIGURE 5.20**

```
                    Display Test Input Data
Record . . . : ITEM

View indicators and input field values.

Field     Value
ITMNUM    111111:
ITMNME    WHOLE MILK :




                                                        Bottom

Press Enter to continue

F3=Exit       F12=Cancel       F14=Display input buffer
```

**FIGURE 5.21**

```
                    Set Test Output Data
Record . . . : ITEM

Type indicators and output field values, press Enter.

Field     Value
ITMNUM    111111:_____
ITMNME    WHOLE MILK:_____
FLD001    ITEM 1111111 — WHOLE MILK — ALREADY EXISTS IN THE DATABASE.






                                                        Bottom

F3=Exit    F12=Cancel
```

FIGURE 5.22

```
 14:01:12                                                    1/15/93
                          ITEM UPDATE SCREEN
           ITEM NUMBER: 111111

            ITEM NAME : WHOLE MILK






                    PRESS F3 TO EXIT THIS DISPLAY



MSG: ITEM 111111 — WHOLE MILK — ALREADY EXISTS IN THE DATABASE.
```

## Creating Menus

Menus are even easier to create than screens. To create a menu, select option 2, Design menus, from the AS/400 Screen Design Aid (SDA) screen (see Figure 5.1). This will result in the Design Menus screen. At this screen, specify the library, file, and member in which to store the menu definition. (All menu definition members have a type of MNUDDS.) Once the information is entered, press ENTER. The Specify Menu Functions screen is displayed. The user would specify **Y** for the Work with menu image and commands option. This will result in the menu definition screen being displayed (Figure 5.23). The title of the screen will actually be the

FIGURE 5.23

```
                          Design Menus
 NEW                        NEW Menu
 Select one of the following:

      1.
      2.
      3.
      4.
      5.
      6.
      7.
      8.
      9.
     10.
 Selection or command _
 F3=Exit              F10=Work with commands    F12=Cancel
 F13=Command area    F20=Reverse                F24=More keys
 Press Help for a list of valid operations.
```

member name specified earlier, followed by the word *Menu*. The example menu member was called NEW; therefore, the screen name is `NEW Menu`. If an inventory functions menu were being defined and the member had been called INVFUNC, the name of the screen would be `INVFUNC Menu`.

The menu definition screen allows the user to change the menu name by simply typing over the old one. Up to ten menu options can be defined on this screen. Move the cursor next to the option number and type the appropriate text that describes the function that will be offered by that menu option.

To define what each option will do, press **F10**. This will bring up the `Define Menu Commands` screen (Figure 5.24). This screen allows the user to enter a CL command that will be executed when an option is chosen. For instance, the first menu option could be `Start PDM`. In this case, the CL command STRPDM would be typed in as the command to be executed. Option 2 could be `Update item`. The command entered at option 2 of the `Define Menu Commands` screen would be CALL ITMUPD. Assuming that the ITMUPD program uses the screen defined earlier, when option 2 is chosen, the `Item Update` screen would be displayed (as in Figure 5.18 without the data fields being filled in).

A system function, a user-defined application program, or a CL job stream can be called and executed from a menu. Moreover, constant text fields can be added to the menu, and all field attribute characters covered earlier in the chapter can be specified for any menu field. Pressing **ENTER** and specifying **Y** at the `Create menu` prompt will result in SDA building a menu.

**FIGURE 5.24**

```
                      Define Menu Commands

  Menu . . . . . . : NEW        Position to menu option . . . . ._ _

  Type commands, press Enter.

  Option Command
  01        _____
            _____
  02        _____
            _____
  03        _____
            _____
  04        _____
            _____
  05        _____
            _____
  06        _____
            _____
  07        _____
            _____
                                                          More...
  F3=Exit    F11=Defined only options    F12=Cancel    F24=More keys
```

## Summary

SDA allows users to define and create display files. Through an easy-to-use, menu-driven interface, SDA allows the user to define and control the display characteristics of constant text fields, system variable fields, and data fields. Based on the characteristics specified by the user, SDA then creates the appropriate DDS specifications and stores them in a new type of object called a display record. This source definition of the screen is then compiled into a display file. The display file contains the machine-understandable definition of the screen and is the object that will be used by application programs.

The display file can also be tested using SDA. The SDA test facility allows the user to "send" the screen to a workstation display just as it would appear if an application had sent it. The user can then enter information in areas defined for input. All defined edits and audits will be performed. In addition, the contents of the buffer that would be passed back to the application program can be displayed. The test utility also lets a user set the values of output fields and then send the screen. In this way, the user can see the screen as it would appear with data.

SDA also provides a facility to quickly define menus that can contain up to ten options. These options can be used to invoke system and application programs, as well as other screens and menus.

## LAB EXERCISE

This lab exercise will create a screen that allows the user to pass salary and state information to the CL program PAY. (PAY was used as an example in Chapter 4.) After the screen is created, the CL program will be modified to display and receive the screen. This will be done by changing the program's logic flow and adding CL commands that identify and manipulate a display file.

To create a member to hold the screen source definition:

1. Create a new file called PAYSRC with an attribute of PF-SRC within YOURLIBXX.

2. Create a new member called PAYDSPF with a type of DSPF in file PAYSRC.

To create a display file with SDA:

1. Type **STRSDA** at any command line and press ENTER.

2. Select option 1, Design screens, from the AS/400 Screen Design Aid (SDA) screen.

3. Specify **YOURLIBXX**, **PAYSRC**, and **PAYDSPF** at the appropriate prompts.

4. On the Work with Display Records screen, specify **1** in the Opt column to add a record and enter **NETSALARY** as the record name. Press ENTER.

5. At the Add New Record screen, make sure **RECORD** is specified for the Type prompt and press ENTER.

6. On the Netsalary Work screen:

    a. Move to the second line, column 5, and type **\*time**.

    b. On the second line, at column 65, type **\*date**.

    c. Move to the third line, column 26, and type **'Net Salary Calculation'**.

    d.    Move to line 7, column 10, and type **'Please enter gross salary and state'**.

    e.    Move to line 10, column 17, and type **'Gross Salary:'**. On line 10, at column 32, type **+9(6)**.

    f.    Move to line 14, column 24, and type **'State:'**. On line 14, at column 32, type **+BB**.

    g.    Move to line 20, column 19, and type **'Net Salary:'**. On line 20, at column 32, type **+6(6)**.

    h.    Move to line 23, column 10, and type **'To exit, enter -1 in the state field and press Enter'**.

    i.    Press ENTER.

    j.    Place an asterisk in line 23's constant text field's attribute field (column 10) and press ENTER.

    k.    On the Select Field Keywords screen, specify **Y** for the Display attributes prompt and press ENTER.

    l.    On the Select Display Attributes screen, specify **Y** for the High intensity prompt. Press ENTER. Press F3 to exit.

    m.    Place an asterisk in the Net Salary data field's attribute field (line 20, column 32) and press ENTER.

    n.    On the Select Field Keywords screen, specify **Y** for the Editing keywords prompt and press ENTER.

    o.    On the Select Editing Keywords screen, specify **4** for the Edit code prompt and **$** for the Replace leading zeros with prompt. Press ENTER. Press F3 to exit.

    p.    Place an asterisk in the State data field's attribute field (line 14, column 32) and press ENTER.

    q.    On the Select Field Keywords screen, specify **Y** for the Validity check prompt and press ENTER.

    r.    On the Valid Check Keywords screen, specify **'FL' 'NY' 'WA' '-1'** at the Values list prompt. Press ENTER. Press F3 to exit.

    s.    Press ENTER.

    t.    Press F3.

7.    At the Exit SDA Work Screen, select option 1.

8.    At the Work with Display Records screen, press F3.

9.    Specify **Y** to both the Save DDS source and Create display file prompts, then press ENTER twice. This will create the display file object that can be used in the CL program.

10.    Exit SDA by pressing F3.

11.    Start PDM and look at objects under YOURLIBXX. Notice the new object PAYDSPF with a type of *FILE and an attribute of DSPF. This object was created by SDA in step 9.

12.    Also look at members under PAYSRC. Notice the new member PAYDSPF. Display the member. This is the DDS that SDA generated based on the specifications made at the SDA Netsalary Work screen in step 5.

To create a CL program to send and receive a screen:

1.  Create a new member called PAY with type equal to CLP under PAYSRC and enter the following CL program:

```
*************** Beginning of data ****************************************
0001.00 /**********************************************************************/
0002.00 /* THIS PROGRAM CALCULATES NET SALARY.                               */
0003.00 /* LINE 26 SENDS THE INITIAL BLANK SCREEN TO THE WORKSTATION DISPLAY. */
0004.00 /* AFTER THE SCREEN HAS BEEN SENT BACK TO THE PROGRAM, LINE 27        */
0005.00 /*     DETERMINES WHETHER THE USER WISHES TO PERFORM ANOTHER NET      */
0006.00 /*     SALARY CALCULATION. THIS IS DONE BY CHECKING THE VALUE OF THE  */
0007.00 /*     SCREEN'S STATE FIELD. IF THE USER HAS ENTERED A -1 IN THE      */
0008.00 /*     STATE FIELD THEN NONE OF THE CALCULATIONS BETWEEN THE DO AND   */
0009.00 /*     THE ENDDO STATEMENTS WILL BE PERFORMED AND THE PROGRAM WILL END.*/
0010.00 /* LINES 29 AND 30 SET PROGRAM VARIABLES EQUAL TO THE SCREEN VALUES.  */
0011.00 /* LINES 31 THRU 38 CALCULATE NET SALARY AFTER FEDERAL WITHHOLDING.   */
0012.00 /*.LINES 39 THRU 47 CALCULATE NET SALARY AFTER NY STATE WITHHOLDING.  */
0013.00 /* LINE 48 SETS THE SCREEN'S NETSALARY OUTPUT FIELD EQUAL TO THE      */
0014.00 /*     RESULT OF THE CALCULATION.                                     */
0015.00 /* LINE 49 SENDS THE SCREEN WITH THE ORIGINAL INPUT VALUES AND THE    */
0016.00 /*     CALCULATED NET SALARY VALUE BACK TO THE WORKSTATION DISPLAY.   */
0017.00 /* WHEN THE USER PRESSES ENTER AND THE SCREEN IS SENT BACK TO THE     */
0018.00 /*     PROGRAM, LINE 50 SENDS CONTROL BACK TO LINE 27, WHERE IT IS    */
0019.00 /*     DETERMINED IF ANOTHER NET SALARY SHOULD BE CALCULATED.         */
0020.00 /**********************************************************************/
0021.00 START:      PGM
0022.00             DCL        VAR(&NETSAL) TYPE(*DEC) LEN(6)
0023.00             DCL        VAR(&SAL) TYPE(*DEC) LEN(6)
0024.00             DCL        VAR(&STATE) TYPE(*CHAR) LEN(2)
0025.00             DCLF       FILE(PAYDSPF) RCDFMT(NETSALARY)
0026.00             SNDRCVF RCDFMT(NETSALARY)
0027.00 LOOP:       IF COND(&FLD002 *NE '-1') +
0028.00             THEN(DO)
0029.00                 CHGVAR VAR(&SAL) VALUE(&FLD001)
0030.00                 CHGVAR VAR(&STATE) VALUE(&FLD002)
0031.00                 IF COND(&SAL > 50000) +
0032.00                     THEN(CHGVAR VAR(&NETSAL) VALUE(&SAL * .65))
0033.00                 IF COND(&SAL > 25000 *AND &SAL <= 50000) +
0034.00                     THEN(CHGVAR VAR(&NETSAL) VALUE(&SAL * .75))
0035.00                 IF COND(&SAL > 15000 *AND &SAL <= 25000) +
0036.00                     THEN(CHGVAR VAR(&NETSAL) VALUE(&SAL * .85))
0037.00                 IF COND(&SAL <= 15000) +
0038.00                     THEN(CHGVAR VAR(&NETSAL) VALUE(&SAL))
0039.00                 IF (&STATE = 'NY') +
0040.00                     THEN(DO)
0041.00                         IF COND(&SAL > 25000) +
0042.00                             THEN(CHGVAR VAR(&NETSAL) +
0043.00                                 VALUE(&NETSAL - (&SAL * .10)))
0044.00                         IF COND(&SAL < 25000) +
0045.00                             THEN(CHGVAR VAR(&NETSAL) +
0046.00                                 VALUE(&NETSAL - (&SAL * .05)))
0047.00                     ENDDO
0048.00                 CHGVAR VAR(&FLD003) VALUE(&NETSAL)
0049.00                 SNDRCVF RCDFMT(NETSALARY)
0050.00                 GOTO LOOP
0051.00             ENDDO
0052.00 END:        ENDPGM
*************** End of data ****************************************
```

Notice the new DCLF command in line 25. This is used to identify a display file in a CL program. The SNDRCVF command in line 26 will display the screen at the workstation that calls the program and halt execution of the program. When ENTER is pressed, any information in the input fields will be passed back to the program, and execution will begin at the statement following the SNDRCVF command.

2. Exit, save, and compile the member.

3. At any command line, type **CALL PAY** and press ENTER.

4. At the SDA-defined screen, type **10000** as gross salary and **FL** as the state. Press ENTER.

5. Notice that net salary is calculated and displayed (with a leading $) in the output field.

6. Enter other gross salary figures and states. Check that the validation is being done for the State field by entering invalid state codes.

7. When you have finished, enter **-1** in the State field and press ENTER.

---

**REVIEW QUESTIONS**

1. What is a display file?

2. Give three examples of system variable fields.

3. What are the two ways that data fields can be defined?

4. What is a display record? What is its relationship to a display file?

5. What are attribute characters, and where are they specified on a screen?

6. What are display attributes? Provide examples.

7. What is stored in a source physical file member with a type of MNUDDS?

8. Describe the fields that would be created by the following definitions:

   +B(6)

   +6(3)

   +3(6)

   +I

   +9(3,2)

9. What other system utility allows users to define screens through an easy-to-use menu interface?

---

**DISCUSSION QUESTIONS**

1. Compare creating screen definitions by entering DDS specifications through SEU to specifying screen definitions with SDA.

2. Describe the capabilities of the SDA test facility.

# AS/400 Database Management

# 6

**Overview**

Data management is an essential component of all computer systems. How data is stored and accessed on a computer will affect every program and user. This chapter will cover how to define AS/400 data files.

After finishing this chapter, you will understand:

- Data definition languages
- The difference between logical, physical, and source data files
- The capabilities of DDS and IDDU
- What a record format is

You also will be able to:

- Define files and record formats
- Specify field definitions
- Specify field edits and audits
- Load data into a file using DFU

## Databases

A *database management system* (DBMS) is a collection of programs that allows a user to create, store, and access data in a database. A database is made up of groups of related data. A DBMS provides utilities that allow users to define individual data elements, group the related data elements, and build relationships between data groups. A user-friendly DBMS will also provide functions to easily enter, change, and retrieve the stored data.

Another key feature of a DBMS is that it protects data. Programs in the DBMS can back up data and, in the case of processing errors, can reverse incorrect updates. A DBMS also provides efficient access to data and ensures the accuracy and integrity of all data contained within the database.

As mentioned, databases are groups of related data. As an example, imagine a dairy that needs to store three major groups of information.

*Item* information is data about each product produced at the dairy. For instance, each item has a name (skim milk, 1% lowfat milk, egg nog, and so on) and an item number.

*Batch* information is stored regarding each group of product processed. The expiration date of milk depends on when it is processed. All milk received on the same day is processed together and identified with a batch number. Therefore, the batch has an expiration date. The government also requires that extensive information be kept on the processing of all food products. Since each batch is processed individually, the processing data (like the temperature at which the batch was stored) and expiration date are included in the batch record.

*Carton* information is stored for each container of product sold. Each container is identified by a unique serial number. The specific information about the container includes the container amount (pint, quart, gallon, and so on) and the store it was sent to.

Figure 6.1 shows the three groups. Each group would also contain individual data records. Figures 6.2, 6.3, and 6.4 are examples of the data each group contains.

**FIGURE 6.1**

**Three Groups of Data**

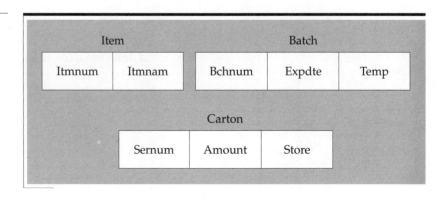

**FIGURE 6.2**
**Item Data**

ITEM

| Itmnum | Itmnam |
|--------|--------|
| 111111 | Whole milk |
| 888888 | Skim milk |
| 666666 | 1% lowfat milk |
| 444444 | Chocolate milk |
| ⋮ | ⋮ |
| 222222 | 2% lowfat milk |

**FIGURE 6.3**
**Batch Data**

BATCH

| Bchnum | Expdte | Temp |
|--------|--------|------|
| 1234 | 10/23/92 | 45 |
| 2345 | 09/30/93 | 38 |
| 5678 | 05/18/90 | 42 |
| 3456 | 08/03/92 | 44 |
| ⋮ | ⋮ | ⋮ |
| 6789 | 01/23/89 | 40 |

**FIGURE 6.4**
**Carton Data**

| CARTON | | |
| Sernum | Amount | Store |
| --- | --- | --- |
| A36SS234 | Half gallon | 8612745 |
| J836H527 | Pint | 9370397 |
| F838938D | Quart | 8937626 |
| 5GDQ3752 | Gallon | 2894628 |
| M7462650 | Quart | 8458532 |
| FY86DY83 | Half pint | 2894628 |
| ⋮ | ⋮ | ⋮ |
| 87Q83J93 | Gallon | 1274007 |

## Relational Databases

In general, relational DBMSs are user friendly and easy to learn. You'll be pleased to know that in keeping with its goal of user friendliness, the AS/400 employs a relational database to store all data.

The two major characteristics of a relational model are that all groups of data are viewed as tables, and relationships between data groups are established through shared fields.

Each row in a table is comparable to a record, and each column is a field. The tables can have a key, and each row can be referenced by the value contained in the key field.

So in a relational database, each group of our dairy database would be considered a table. If you wished to store and access carton information, you need only to set up carton as a table and with a key field of carton number.

To relate information between different tables, the relational model uses duplicate data elements. For instance, if the dairy worker wanted to retrieve the expiration date and storage temperature for a particular carton, the carton and batch tables would need to share a common field. One way this could be solved is to define a batch number field in the carton table (Figure 6.5). When data from the two tables is needed, a JOIN using the shared field BCHNUM from both tables would be specified. The relational DBMS would search through the carton and batch records and join the rows that have the same batch number.

**FIGURE 6.5**
**A Relational Database Implementation**

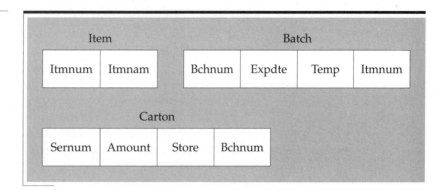

All database management systems offer some capability to define data structures and manipulate the data contained in those structures. Generally, these features are called the *data definition language* (DDL) and the *data manipulation language* (DML). The AS/400 provides several different ways to define, modify, and view data.

In terms of DDL functions, the AS/400 provides two ways to define data. Data can be defined *internally* or *externally*. Internally defined data is defined within application programs using a programming language's data definition commands or SQL (Structured Query Language) commands. On the AS/400, a file could be defined using RPG, COBOL, or any of the other supported programming languages.

Externally defined files are defined outside application programs using a DDL. On the AS/400, files can be defined externally using SQL, IDDU (Interactive Data Definition Utility), or DDS (Data Description Specifications).

SQL commands can define data both externally—through a feature called interactive SQL—and as mentioned earlier, internally—by embedding the commands in an application program. SQL also has data manipulation capability. In addition to commands that define data structures, there are commands to load, view, and modify data.

IDDU is a menu-driven data definition utility. Through a series of menus and screens, IDDU provides options and prompts that enable the user to supply information necessary to define data on the AS/400. After the information has been gathered, IDDU generates and compiles DDS source code for the data.

DDS is strictly a definition language. It contains commands that allow a user to define:

- File structures

- Individual field characteristics

- Field edits and audits

Though IDDU generates DDS code, it is limited in the DDS commands it offers. Furthermore, because IDDU is menu driven, it does not offer the flexibility of PDM and SEU in terms of updating. For these reasons, this chapter will confine itself to discussing DDS for file definition on the AS/400. Manipulating data on the AS/400—another feature of most DBMSs—is handled either by

AS/400 utilities other than DDS or by application programs. The AS/400's data manipulation tool, DFU (Data File Utility), will be covered at the end of this chapter.

## Physical and Logical Data Files

A DBMS will also usually offer three ways to view a database. There is a physical view, a logical view, and the capability to build multiple user views of the data. What is traditionally called the physical view of data is hidden from the AS/400 user because of the AS/400's single-level approach to storage. The user does not know on what disk, track, or sector the data is being stored. In addition, any indices or specific location addresses are used internally by the DBMS and are not readily available to the user. However, DDS does provide a global view of all the data as files and allows construction of individual views. This is achieved through physical and logical files.

Physical files contain the definition of individual tables/files. In addition to a file definition, data physical files include an access path to the data (a key). The data itself is stored in members belonging to the data physical file. Physical files provide an overall view of the data.

Logical files also define a file. Logical files, however, only reference fields previously defined in physical files. A logical file can be defined with fields from a single physical file or a combination of fields from many physical files. In this way, unique views of the data can be built. Logical files do not have data members. When creating logical files, there is no data redundancy; they contain only a definition and an access path to physical file data members. The logical file's usefulness is that it contains a different definition (from the physical file) regarding how to access the data.

Physical and logical files are created by compiling source physical file members. These members contain the DDS statements that define the file's fields and record formats. Source physical file members can be defined with a type of LF or PF (logical file or physical file). This member type determines the file attribute (physical or logical) that will be created when the member is compiled.

For instance, from our dairy example, each group of data—item, batch, and carton—would be defined by DDS statements contained in a source physical file member. The fields for each file would be as shown in Figure 6.5, and the library, files, and members to hold the file definitions would look like Figure 6.6.

Compiling the file definition members would result in three new physical files being created, each having an empty member with no type (Figure 6.7). The new physical files would contain the compiled file definitions, and the empty members will eventually hold the data.

A logical file could be defined—say, BATCART—to contain fields from both the batch and carton files. DDS commands would specify a join for batch and carton records that share the same batch number. The DDS could also limit the fields in the logical file to expiration date (from BATCH) and carton number, batch number, and store (from CARTON). The DDS would be stored in the source physical file member with a type of LF called BATCART (Figure 6.8). When BATCART is compiled, a new object with a type of *FILE and an

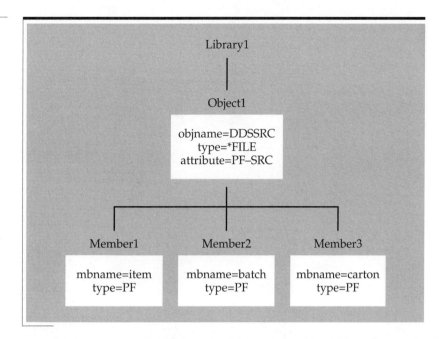

FIGURE 6.6
**AS/400 Source Member Organization**

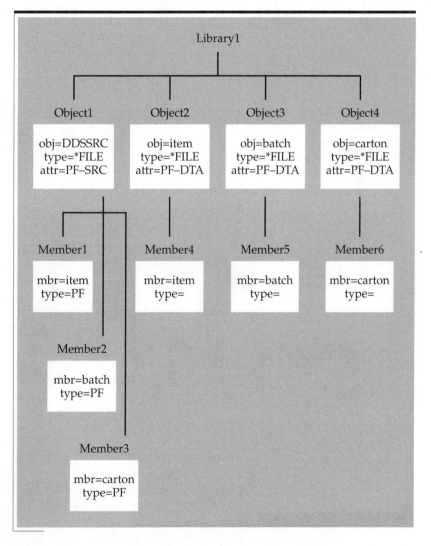

FIGURE 6.7
**Source Member and File Organization After Compiling**

FIGURE 6.8
**Logical File Source
Member**

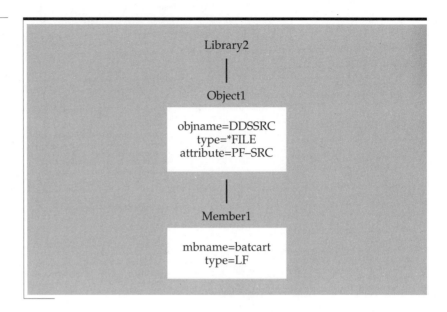

FIGURE 6.8
**Logical File Source
Member**

attribute of LF is created (Figure 6.9). A logical file does not have any members. Logical files simply "point" to the physical files' member(s) (that contain the data) and specify how to access that data. The DDS also specifies how the fields and records will be arranged within the logical file.

FIGURE 6.9
**Logical File Source
Member and Logical File**

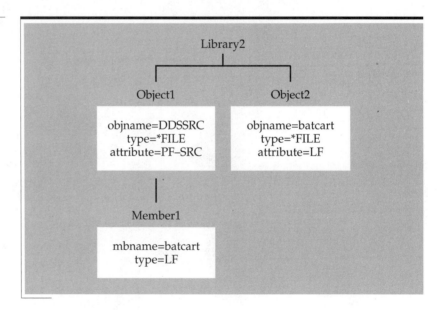

## Creating a Physical File

Creating a physical or logical file starts with creating a source physical file member to hold the DDS definition. PDM can be used to create a library, a source physical file, and a member with type of PF or LF. (See Chapters 2 and 3 for instructions on creating these objects.) For this chapter's purposes, we assume the source physical file INVSRC has been created in library YOURLIBXX. Within INVSRC, create a member called INVDATA with a type of PF.

A few words about DDS before we cover individual commands and syntax. DDS is a semipositional language, meaning that many commands and values must be placed in certain column positions on the line. Unlike a free format language, DDS is strict about where on the line, for instance, the name of a field is defined. Other optional specifications, such as edits and audits (an example is a specification that checks that any value entered is greater than 0), are not as strictly governed.

When defining either a physical or a logical file, there are also certain rules that must be followed. For instance, a physical file can have only one record format (e.g., a layout and definitions of individual fields) defined, and the record format must contain at least one field definition.

For our example, we are going to define a file that holds information about a grocer's inventory and suppliers. The fields that make up the file will be as follows:

| Field Name | Field Description |
| --- | --- |
| ITMNUM | Item Number |
| ITMNME | Item Name |
| EOQ | Economic Order Quantity |
| QTYNST | Quantity in Stock |
| REORDP | Reorder Point |
| UNTPRC | Unit Price |
| SUPPL | Supplier Name |
| SUPADD | Supplier Address |
| SUPCTY | Supplier City |
| SUPST | Supplier State |
| SUPZP | Supplier Zip Code |

EOQ and REORDP are fields needed to determine when and how much product to order. REORDP is the quantity of product in stock that, when reached, signifies that more product should be ordered. Based on factors such as time required for delivery and item consumption rate, each item's reorder point is calculated and assigned by the user. EOQ is the optimal amount of an item that should be reordered. This is usually based on consumption rate, shelf life, and order quantity discounts offered by the supplier.

## DDS

By using DDS, a programmer gets several advantages inherent to an externally described file. If a file is described internally, each program that accesses that file must also include a definition of the format or view of the data that will be used. With DDS, that format can be defined once, outside the program, and any program can use that definition. This saves the programmer from having to reenter the definition for each program. Further, any changes to the file structure are made in the DDS definition. Nothing in the programs is affected. Rather than going into multiple programs and changing each internally defined format, the DDS definition provides one stored copy of the definition that can be accessed and updated. This greatly speeds up and simplifies the updating process and reduces the chance of mistakes.

DDS file specifications are entered into a source physical member and can span one or more lines. Each line is broken up into several different areas. All positional entries are specified between columns 1 and 44. Columns 45 through 80 are considered the function area.

The three levels of definition for a physical file are file, record, and field. Respectively, these levels determine whether the keywords specified affect the entire file, a record, or an individual field.

An example of a file level specification would be whether records with duplicate keys are allowed in the file. Moreover, if duplicate keys are allowed, then another file level specification needs to be made regarding the order that duplicate records will be processed; that is, is the first duplicated record written to the file the first record that is printed out, or is the last duplicated record entered the first printed? File level specifications are designated by entering keywords in the function area of a line before all record or field level specifications.

Figure 6.10, line 3, is an example of a file level specification. By having a keyword in column 45 as the first specification record and not associating it with an individual record or field, it signifies that the keyword applies to the entire file. The keyword UNIQUE specifies that each record in the file must have a unique key value.

**FIGURE 6.10**

```
 Columns . . . :  1   71              Edit              YOURLIBXX/INVSRC
 SEU==> _____ INVDATA
 FMT A* .....A*. 1 ...+... 2 ...+... 3 ...+... 4 ...+... 5 ...+... 6 ...+... 7
 *************** Beginning of data ****************************************
 0001.00     *      THIS IS A DDS PHYSICAL FILE DEFINITION
 0002.00     *
 0003.00                                      UNIQUE
 0004.00            R INVFMT                   TEXT('INVENTORY FORMAT')
 0005.00              ITMNUM       6P 0        COLHDG('ITEM' 'NUMBER')
 0006.00                                       TEXT('ITEM NUMBER')
 0007.00                                       CHECK(ME)
 0008.00              ITMNME      15           COLHDG('ITEM' 'NAME')
 0009.00                                       TEXT('ITEM NAME')
 0010.00              EOQ          2P 0        COLHDG('EOQ' 'AMOUNT')
 0011.00                                       TEXT('EOQ AMOUNT')
 0012.00                                       COMP(GT 0)
 0013.00                                       CHECK(ME)
 0014.00              QTYNST       2P 0        COLHDG('QUANTITY' 'IN STOCK')
 0015.00                                       TEXT('QUANTITY IN STOCK')
 0016.00                                       COMP(GE 0)
 0017.00                                       CHECK(ME)
 0018.00              REORDP       2P 0        COLHDG('REORDER' 'POINT')
 0019.00                                       TEXT('REORDER POINT')
 0020.00                                       CHECK(ME)
 0021.00              UNTPRC       4P 2        COLHDG('UNIT' 'PRICE')
 0022.00                                       TEXT('UNIT PRICE')
 0023.00                                       CHECK(ME)
 0024.00              SUPPL       20           COLHDG('SUPPLIER' 'NAME')
 0025.00                                       TEXT('SUPPLIER NAME')
 0026.00                                       CHECK(ME)
 0027.00              SUPPADD     20           COLHDG('SUPPLIER' 'ADDRESS')
 0028.00                                       TEXT('SUPPLIER ADDRESS')
 0029.00                                       CHECK(ME)
 0030.00              SUPCTY      15           COLHDG('SUPPLIER' 'CITY')
 0031.00                                       TEXT('SUPPLIER CITY')
 0032.00                                       CHECK(ME)
 0033.00              SUPST        2           COLHDG('STATE')
 0034.00                                       TEXT('STATE')
 0035.00                                       CHECK(ME)
 0036.00              SUPZP        5P 0        COLHDG('ZIPCODE')
 0037.00                                       TEXT('ZIP CODE')
 0038.00                                       CHECK(MF)
 0039.00            K ITMNUM
 **************** End of data ********************************************
```

Line 4 shows a record level specification. An R in column 17 signifies that the specification is for a record, and the name of the record format is entered in columns 19 through 28. In the function area, the keyword TEXT is specified. TEXT allows the user to specify descriptive information about the record format. When the record format is used in a program, the text will be included in the program as documentation. The syntax of the TEXT command requires enclosing the description with single quotes and parentheses. The TEXT keyword can also be used for field level specifications.

The remaining entries in Figure 6.10 are all examples of field level specifications. The field name is specified in the same column positions as the record name. Fields require a length specification. Positions 30 through 34 are reserved for length entries. Column 35 is reserved for the data type. A blank indicates a character field, and several values (P, S, B, F, H) can be specified for numeric fields. For this example, all numeric fields are specified with a P, meaning packed. If decimal places are needed, the number required is entered in positions 36 and 37.

While typing in the DDS specifications, positioning the cursor at the correct column and entering the data can become a nuisance. SEU supplies a DDS input prompt that will easily position entries in the correct columns. Pressing F4 displays the input prompt. (The type of member determines what prompt will be displayed.) Because this is a physical file member, the DDS prompt will be displayed in the bottom portion of the screen (Figure 6.11). On the second half of the screen, notice a prompt field called Functions. This is where a function keyword, such as UNIQUE or TEXT, would be entered. Press ENTER, and SEU will place the keyword in column 45.

Several other keywords can also be specified for field level edits.

**FIGURE 6.11**

```
Columns . . . : 1 71              Edit              YOURLIBXX/INVSRC
SEU==>                                                         INVDATA
FMT A* ....A*. 1 ...+... 2 ...+... 3 ...+... 4 ...+... 5 ...+... 6 ...+... 7
************* Beginning of data *****************************
0001.00    *      THIS IS A DDS PHYSICAL FILE DEFINITION
0002.00    *
0003.00                                  UNIQUE
0004.00              R INVFMT            TEXT('INVENTORY FORMAT')
0005.00                ITMNUM       6P 0  COLHDG('ITEM' 'NUMBER')
0006.00                                  TEXT('ITEM NUMBER')
0007.00                                  CHECK(ME)
0008.00                ITMNME       15    COLHDG('ITEM' 'NAME')
0009.00                                  TEXT('ITEM NAME')
 Prompt type . . . PF    Sequence number . . .  0003.00

 Name                        Data   Decimal
 Type      Name    Ref  Length  Type   Positions      Use
  _         _      _   ____    _     __            _
 Functions
 Unique _____

 F3=Exit  F4=Prompt  F5=Refresh        F11=Previous record
 F12=Cancel           F23=Select prompt  F24=More keys
```

- **CHECK**. This keyword determines the data that must be entered for a field when the record is being input. There are several options:

    AB (allow blank) means no entry is necessary, and blanks or zeros will be substituted if no data is entered.

    ME (mandatory entry) means at least one character must be entered in the field. A single blank is a valid entry.

    MF (mandatory fill) means all positions in the field must be filled in. (The zip code field is an example of a field that must be entirely filled in.)

- **COMP**. This keyword specifies a comparison to be performed when data is being entered. That data entered must result in the comparison being true. The valid operators include:

    EQ equal

    NE not equal

    LT less than

    LE less than or equal

    GT greater than

    GE greater than or equal

    An example of a COMP specification can be found on line 12 of Figure 6.10. It ensures that any number entered in the EOQ field must be greater than zero.

- **EDTCDE**. This keyword allows the user to control the appearance of numeric and date fields. Various single character and number codes control whether there should be a thousands separator, leading zeros should be suppressed, or a positive or negative sign should be displayed.

- **COLHDG**. This keyword defines the text that will appear as a column heading for the field on data entry or data display screens.

- **RANGE**. This keyword specifies that an audit be performed to check that any entered value is within a range of values. For instance, a date would be made up of separate fields for month, day, and year. A range could be specified for the month field as Range(1 12). Any value that is entered in the month field will be checked. If the value is not from 1 to 12, inclusive, it will not be allowed in the database.

- **VALUES**. This keyword specifies that a check be performed against a specific group of values. Using the month example again, month could be defined as a character field that should contain only the discrete values of 'January', 'February', and so on. To specify this edit, use the VALUES keyword as follows:

VALUES('January' 'February' 'March' 'April' 'May' 'June' 'July' 'August' 'September' 'October' 'November' 'December')

Once all the DDS has been specified, press F3 to exit and save the member (as described in Chapter 3). Compiling the DDS member will create the data physical file and member that will hold the data.

## Logical Files

A logical file contains a different access path to physical file records and fields. A logical file can appear to contain a rearrangement of physical file data fields, a subset of data fields from a single physical file, or information from multiple files. A logical file is usually built to correspond to an individual user's (or group of users') view of the data.

The keywords and procedures to create and define a logical file are much the same as for a physical file. There are, however, some special requirements on referencing fields in the physical files as well as rules on combining multiple physical files.

As a simple logical file example, we will define a logical file, INVACCT, for the INVDATA file. This logical file will correspond to an accountant's view of inventory data. Accountants are concerned with the value of inventory. They are usually not concerned with who supplies the item or what the reorder quantity is.

Accountants need to see an item's number, name, and unit price as well as the quantity in stock. From this information, they can calculate the total dollar value of the current inventory in stock.

To create a logical file, the user must first create a physical file member in which to store the logical file definition. For the INVACCT example, the user would create a physical file member within INVSRC called INVACCT with a type of LF. The DDS shown in Figure 6.12 would then be entered. (Use the browse and copy function to retrieve the INVDATA definition. Then modify the INVDATA definition to match Figure 6.12.)

**FIGURE 6.12**

```
Columns . . . : 1 71          Edit              YOURLIBXX/INVSRC
SEU==>_____ INVACCT
FMT A* .....A*. 1 ...+... 2 ...+... 3 ...+... 4 ...+... 5 ...+... 6 ...+... 7
           ************* Beginning of data *************************
0001.00    *    THIS IS THE LOGICAL FILE THAT DEFINES THE
0002.00    *    ACCOUNTING VIEW OF INVENTORY DATA
0003.00                              UNIQUE
0004.00         R ACCFMT             PFILE(YOURLIBXX/INVDATA)
0005.00                              TEXT('ACCOUNTING FORMAT')
0006.00           ITMNUM
0007.00           ITMNME
0008.00           QTYNST
0009.00           UNTPRC
0010.00         K ITMNUM
0011.00         O QTYNST             COMP(LE 0)
***************** End of data ********************************

F3=Exit  F4=Prompt   F5=Refresh  F9=Retrieve  F10=Cursor
F16=Repeat find      F17=Repeat change        F24=More keys
```

Notice that the logical file also has file, record, and field level specifications. As mentioned, a logical file definition contains many of the same keywords as a physical file. In Figure 6.12 the TEXT keyword defines the new logical file's format text. Using field level keywords in the logical file will override any physical file field definition. For instance, column headings could be redefined for each of the logical file fields using the COLHDG keyword. If no field level keyword is specified, the value defined in the physical file is used.

There are, however, some important differences between logical and physical file definitions. For instance, the record level keyword PFILE is required in a logical file (see line 4 in Figure 6.12). Since a logical file provides a different view of a physical file(s), the physical file(s) must be specified. In the case of a single physical file, this is done through the PFILE keyword.

A new field level specification is also shown in Figure 6.12. Line 11 demonstrates an *omit specification*. The keyword COMP was used earlier as a validity checker. In a logical file, however, it can also be used to select or omit physical file records from the logical file. Entering the letter O in position 17 will define the field level specification as an omit. Line 11 omits any physical file records that have a quantity of zero or less. This was done because accountants are concerned with the value of inventory. If an item has no inventory (that is, its quantity in stock is zero), there is no dollar value for that item's inventory.

Screening out the zero value records could also have been accomplished with a selection. To define a field level specification as a select, enter an S in position 17. If the same function were to be accomplished with a select specification, the COMP condition would be changed to QTYNST GT 0.

All the COMP operands listed for physical files are valid for logical files.

To create the logical file, exit the SEU `Edit` screen and save and compile the member. The accountants would be told that their inventory information is stored in the INVACCT file. They would not even have to know that INVDATA exists. Whenever the logical file INVACCT is requested, the AS/400 database will retrieve data from the physical file defined in the PFILE keyword, INVDATA.

## Joining Files

A more complicated logical file is a *join logical file*. A join logical file can contain information from multiple physical files. Essentially, DDS provides the capability to select and join individual fields from different physical files into one logical file. To demonstrate this capability, the BATCH and CARTON files discussed earlier need to be created. Assuming that the two physical file members called BATCH and CARTON have already been created, DDS in Figure 6.13 and Figure 6.14 would be entered into the two members. Then BATCH and CARTON would be saved and compiled.

Assuming that the logical file member called BATCART in INVSRC and YOURLIBXX already exists, enter the DDS in Figure 6.15.

FIGURE 6.13

```
         ******** Beginning of data ******************************
0001.00    * THIS PHYSICAL FILE IS THE BATCH FILE DDS DEFINITION
0002.00    *
0003.00                              UNIQUE
0004.00         R BCHFMT             TEXT('BATCH FORMAT')
0005.00           BCHNUM      4      COLHDG('BATCH' 'NUMBER')
0006.00                              TEXT('BATCH NUMBER')
0007.00                              CHECK(ME)
0008.00           EXPDTE      6      COLHDG('EXPIRATION' 'DATE')
0009.00                              TEXT('EXPIRATION DATE')
0010.00                              CHECK(ME)
0011.00           TEMP        2      COLHDG('TEMP')
0012.00                              TEXT('TEMPERATURE')
0013.00                              CHECK(ME)
0014.00           ITMNUM      6      COLHDG('ITEM' 'NUMBER')
0015.00                              TEXT('ITEM NUMBER')
0016.00                              CHECK(ME)
0017.00         K BCHNUM
         ************* End of data ******************************
```

FIGURE 6.14

```
         ******** Beginning of data ******************************
0001.00    * THIS PHYSICAL FILE IS THE CARTON FILE DDS DEFINITION
0002.00    *
0003.00                              UNIQUE
0004.00         R CRTFMT             TEXT('CARTON FORMAT')
0005.00           CRTNUM      8      COLHDG('CARTON' 'NUMBER')
0006.00                              TEXT('CARTON NUMBER')
0007.00                              CHECK(ME)
0008.00           AMOUNT     12      COLHDG('CARTON' 'SIZE')
0009.00                              TEXT('CARTON SIZE')
0010.00                              CHECK(ME)
0011.00           STORE       7      COLHDG('STORE' 'CODE')
0012.00                              TEXT('STORE CODE')
0013.00                              CHECK(ME)
0014.00           BCHNUM      4      COLHDG('BATCH' 'NUMBER')
0015.00                              TEXT('BATCH NUMBER')
0016.00                              CHECK(ME)
0017.00         K CRTNUM
         ************* End of data ******************************
```

Notice that several new keywords are needed to define a logical join file. For instance, the JFILE keyword (line 4 in Figure 6.15) identifies the files to be joined. Up to 32 files can be specified. (Warn the local power company before you try to join 32 files! Well, calling the power company isn't really necessary; however, you might want to think twice before doing a join of that size. The resources needed to perform that large of a join could be considerable, and overall system performance might be affected.)

The logical file must also have a *join specification*. The join specification must follow the record specification and is indicated by placing a J in column 17 (line 7 in Figure 6.15). This identifies which files are to be joined and the basis for the join. The keyword JOIN (entered in the function area of the join specification) is used to identify the files to be joined. The JOIN keyword is not required if only two files are specified in the JFILE keyword (since they are the only possible files that can be joined); however, for clarity it is shown in the figure. Notice that library and file names are not used to identify the join files. When files are specified in the JFILE keyword, they are assigned a relative file number. The first file is 1, the next is 2, the file specified after the second is 3, and so forth. Whenever the file needs to be identified, the relative file number can be used instead of the longer file and library names. The join specification on line 7 uses the relative numbers.

**FIGURE 6.15**

```
        ******* Beginning of data ******************************
0001.00  * THIS LOGICAL FILE FOR THE JOIN OF THE BATCH AND CARTON FILES
0002.00  *
0003.00                              UNIQUE
0004.00          R BATCARTFMT        JFILE(YOURLIBXX/CARTON +
0005.00                              YOURLIBXX/BATCH)
0006.00                              TEXT('BATCH FORMAT')
0007.00          J                   JOIN(1 2)
0008.00                              JFLD(BCHNUM BCHNUM)
0009.00            CRTNUM
0010.00            BCHNUM            JREF(1)
0011.00            EXPDTE
0012.00            AMOUNT
0013.00          K CRTNUM
        *************** End of data ****************************
```

The JFLD keyword identifies the field(s) that will be used to join the records. In this case, line 8 specifies that records in the CARTON and BATCH files that share the same value in their batch number fields will be joined. More than one field can be defined as the join condition. This might be necessary if more than one field is needed to uniquely identify a record. For instance, the only way to absolutely distinguish each record in a file may be to check the last name, first name, and phone number fields. If this were the case, any records being joined from two different files should have matching data in all these fields. This could be done by using three JFLD keywords.

The last new keyword is JREF. The JREF keyword is required for any field whose name is specified in more than one file. In the example, BCHNUM is in both the CARTON and BATCH files. It is required to specify from which file the field value is to come. In this example, there is no difference since both fields contain the same value. If, however, two files had a field called DATE—one date field containing an employee's date of hire and another containing the date of last salary increase—specifying would make a difference in the value.

To create the BATCART logical file, save and compile member BATCART.

## Manipulating Data in a File

There are many ways to add, update, and retrieve data from a file. In fact, providing these functions is the purpose of most application programs. All programming languages supported by the AS/400 provide commands to perform these functions. In addition, there is SQL/400, the AS/400's version of SQL (Structured Query Language). SQL is a relational database language that allows users to define and manipulate data. The AS/400 also provides a special utility called DFU (Data File Utility), which provides an even simpler way to enter and change data. Rather than writing a data update program in a programming language or SQL, DFU writes the program for you. Through a series of menus and screens, DFU prompts for information regarding the file to update, the program functions to be included, and the screen format. DFU then creates an update screen and program that can be used to enter, change, or delete data in a file. DFU provides the programmer with a "quick and dirty" way to load test data into files.

## Entering and Saving Data Using Temporary DFU Programs

To start DFU, type in the CL command **STRDFU** at any command line and press ENTER. This will result in the AS/400 Data File Utility (DFU) screen (Figure 6.16). This display allows users to create permanent or temporary programs to manipulate data in the database.

FIGURE 6.16

```
            AS/400 Data File Utility (DFU)

  Select one of the following:

      1.  Run a DFU program
      2.  Create a DFU program
      3.  Change a DFU program
      4.  Delete a DFU program
      5.  Update data using temporary program










  Selection or command
  ===>_____

  F3=Exit      F4=Prompt      F9=Retrieve      F12=Cancel
```

As an example, let's create a temporary program to add data to the inventory file we just defined. Choose option 5 and press ENTER. The Update Data Using Temporary Program screen will be displayed (Figure 6.17). At this screen, identify the inventory data file, as shown in Figure 6.17, and press ENTER. DFU will begin creating a program that allows a user to change or enter data to the file. After the program has been created, DFU will automatically execute it, and an update screen will be displayed (Figure 6.18).

**FIGURE 6.17**

```
                  Update Data Using Temporary Program
Type choices, press Enter.

Data file . . . . . .     INVDATA    Name, F4 for list
  Library . . . . . .     YOURLIBXX Name, *LIBL, *CURLIB
Member. . . . . . . .     INVDATA    Name, *FIRST, F4 for list














F3=Exit       F4=Prompt       F12=Cancel
```

**FIGURE 6.18**

```
WORK WITH DATA IN A FILE                 Mode . . . . . : ENTRY
Format . . . . :    INVFMT              File . . . . : INVDATA

ITEM NUMBER:          ____
ITEM NAME:            _____
EOQ AMOUNT:           ___
QUANTITY IN STOCK:    ___
REORDER POINT:        ___
UNIT PRICE:           _____
SUPPLIER NAME:        _____
SUPPLIER ADDRESS:     _____
CITY:                 _____
STATE:                __
ZIPCODE:              _____




F3=Exit       F5=Refresh      F6=Select format
F9=Insert     F10=Entry       F11=Change
```

Since the data member from the last chapter is empty, the program defaults to *entry mode*. Entry mode allows a user to append records to the end of the file. The update screen will have input areas for each field defined by the file's DDS. The input area is designated by underscores to the right of the field name, and the size of the area is defined by the DDS. To add a record to the file, fill in the fields as shown in Figure 6.19 and press F9 to insert. This will bring up another blank entry screen where another record can be inserted.

**FIGURE 6.19**

```
WORK WITH DATA IN A FILE                    Mode . . . . : ENTRY
  Format . . . . :     INVFMT                File . . . . : INVDATA

  ITEM NUMBER:          1
  ITEM NAME:            turnip
  EOQ AMOUNT:           25
  QUANTITY IN STOCK:    43
  REORDER POINT:        50
  UNIT PRICE:           22
  SUPPLIER NAME:        American Turnip Corp
  SUPPLIER ADDRESS:     101 Vegetable Lane
  CITY:                 Bangor
  STATE:                ME
  ZIPCODE:              11111




  F3=Exit        F5=Refresh       F6=Select format
  F9=Insert      F10=Entry        F11=Change
```

To exit and save the new data, press **F3**. This will bring up the
End Data Entry screen (Figure 6.20), which displays information on
the changes, additions, and deletions that were made by the DFU
program. Enter **Y** at the End data entry prompt and press **ENTER**.
At this point, DFU will create an audit report that contains the
changed data and other audit report information (Figure 6.21).

**FIGURE 6.20**

```
                       End Data Entry
  Number of records processed

     Added . . . . . :      1
     Changed . . . . :      0
     Deleted . . . . :      0



  Type choice, press Enter.

     End data entry . . . . . . . Y      Y=Yes, N=No







  F3=Exit        F12=Cancel
```

**FIGURE 6.21**

```
  5738SS1   V2R1M0 910524    AUDIT LOG              9/23/92 13:37:56   PAGE 1


  Library/File . . . . .      YOURLIBXX/INVDATA
  Member . . . . . . . .      INVDATA
  Job Title . . . . . .       WORK WITH DATA IN A FILE


          ITEM       ITEM       EOQ      QUANTITY    REORDER    UNIT
          NUMBER     NAME       AMOUNT   IN STOCK    POINT      PRICE
  Added     1        turnip     25         43          50        .22


          SUPPLIER            SUPPLIER             CITY      STATE ZIPCODE
          NAME                ADDRESS

  American Turnip Corp  101 Vegetable Lane  Bangor     ME     11111

              1 Records Added
              0 Records Changed
              0 Records Deleted
      * * * * E N D  O F  D F U  A U D I T  R E P O R T * * * * * * * *
```

## Changing Data Using DFU

To change existing information, invoke DFU again. Because the file now contains data, the DFU program will default to change mode. The change screen will contain only the key field(s) (Figure 6.22). The user would enter the key value for the particular record to be changed. To change the turnip record, type **1** in the ITEM NUMBER input area and then press **F11**, the Change option. The turnip record would appear with all the previously defined field values displayed. To change any of the data, move the cursor to the field to be changed and type over the current value. For instance, say two turnips were sold this week (probably the biggest run on turnips all year). This means the quantity in stock has decreased to 41. Move the cursor to the QUANTITY IN STOCK field and type **41**, the new stock quantity. The

**FIGURE 6.22**

```
     WORK WITH DATA IN A FILE          Mode . . . . . : CHANGE
     Format . . . . :  INVFMT          File . . . . . : INVDATA

     ITEM NUMBER:       ____



















     F3=Exit        F5=Refresh      F6=Select format
     F9=Insert      F10=Entry       F11=Change
```

new data is not inserted into the file when the old value is typed over. To make the change to the file, press F11. A blank change screen will reappear (Figure 6.22). This means that the data has been inserted into the file. To verify that the change was made, type item number 1 again and press ENTER. The turnip record will appear with the new value, 41, in the QUANTITY IN STOCK field.

Several other functions can be performed from the change screen by pressing the appropriate function key.

To *delete* a record, enter the key value for the record to be deleted and then press F23. The data fields and the values for the record specified will appear. Pressing F23 a second time will confirm that this is the record to be deleted, and the record will be deleted.

To *insert* data into the file press F9. A blank screen with all the file's fields will be displayed. Enter field values for the new record and press F9. The new record would be appended to the file and the index updated accordingly. If the file has no key, insert mode would be the same as entry mode—the record would simply be appended to the end of the file. The user can switch between insert, entry, and change modes by pressing F9, F10, and F11, respectively.

For files with multiple formats, the format being used can be changed. Pressing F6 (select format) will result in a list of valid formats for the file being displayed. Select the format by typing 1 next to the format name and pressing ENTER.

As an exercise, enter the records in Figure 6.23 into the file using a temporary DFU program.

**FIGURE 6.23**
**Sample Records**

| ITEM NUMBER: | 2 | 3 | 51 |
|---|---|---|---|
| ITEM NAME: | cantaloupe | radish | onion |
| EOQ AMOUNT: | 15 | 75 | 50 |
| QTY. IN STOCK: | 15 | 0 | 20 |
| REORDER PT.: | 10 | 50 | 40 |
| UNIT PRICE: | 72 | 6 | 350 |
| SUPPLIER NAME: | Amalgamated Fruits | Radishes 'R Us | Stinky's |
| SUPPLIER ADDRESS: | 1 Cherry Blossom Ct | 1 Dirt St | Pea-Yew Dr |
| CITY: | Walla Walla | Larchmont | Vadalia |
| STATE: | WA | TX | GA |
| ZIPCODE: | 99999 | 44444 | 33333 |

## Summary

Data is a cornerstone of modern business. The complexity and the amount of data stored by businesses have grown in proportion to the importance of the data. To store and protect data, database management systems have been widely adopted. These collections of programs enable users to define different types of relationships between their data and access the data in a fast and efficient manner.

The AS/400 provides a variety of tools to perform both data definition and data manipulation. PDM allows users to create members that will hold file definitions (process 1 in Figure 6.24). The primary data definition tool is DDS. The user enters DDS source code specifications into a source physical file member with SEU (process 2 in

Figure 6.24). The member is then compiled through PDM (option 14), and an AS/400 file and data member are created (see process 2 in Figure 6.24). The AS/400 also provides ease-of-use features such as prompts and on-line help.

Further control over data is provided through logical files. Different views can be built to match individual users' data needs. Rather than accessing and retrieving data from multiple physical files, a single logical file can be created that appears to combine all the needed data into one file. In actuality, no data is duplicated, but user access to the data is easier.

DFU provides a quick and easy way to add and update data to AS/400 files. These data files are updated by DFU-generated programs (Figure 6.25). Data files are not updated by DFU. Rather, DFU creates programs, based on user specifications (see process 1 in Figure 6.25). These programs access and display data to the user, as well as receive new data and update the file (see process 2 in Figure 6.25). DFU acts as an application program generator, and the data is updated according to the mode in which the program is run.

Though DFU is a quick way to generate update programs, any significant amount of data would be burdensome to load through a DFU-generated program. DFU is primarily used for setting up test data.

**FIGURE 6.24**

**The Process Required to Create an AS/400 Data File and Member**

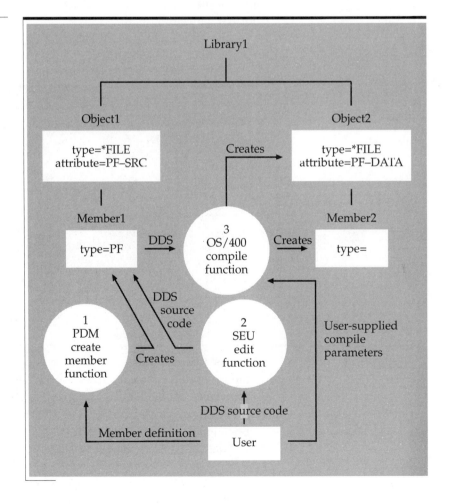

FIGURE 6.25

**Creating and Using
DFU-Generated Update
Programs**

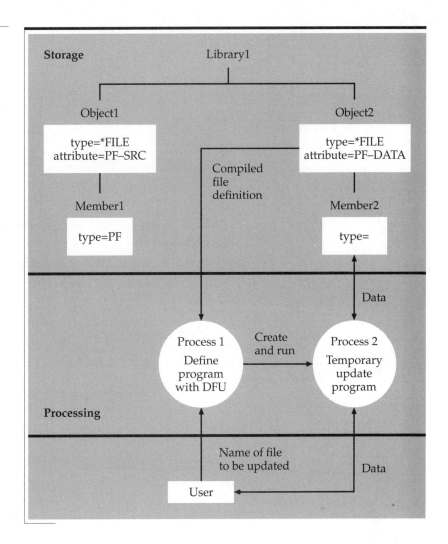

This database lab exercise will create a joined logical file of three physical files. The three files will be the BATCH, CARTON, and ITEM files mentioned in the chapter. The logical file will contain each carton's number, the store it was sent to, date of expiration, and type of milk.

1.  If the BATCH and CARTON files have not been created, create the members in YOURLIBXX within INVSRC, enter the DDS source (see Figures 6.13 and 6.14 for the DDS source), and compile the members.

2.  If the members ITEM (with a type of PF) and ITBATCAR (with a type of LF) in YOURLIBXX within INVSRC have not been created, create them now. (Use CRTMBR, the CL program created in the second lab exercise in Chapter 3, to create these new members.)

3.   Enter the following DDS into member ITEM:

```
*************** Beginning of data ****************************
0001.00    *     THIS PHYSICAL FILE IS THE ITEM FILE DDS DEFINITION
0002.00    *
0003.00                              UNIQUE
0004.00            R ITMFMT          TEXT('ITEM FORMAT')
0005.00              ITMNUM   6      COLHDG('ITEM' 'NUMBER')
0006.00                              TEXT('ITEM NUMBER')
0007.00                              CHECK(ME)
0008.00              ITMNAM  15      COLHDG('ITEM' 'NAME')
0009.00                              TEXT('ITEM NAME')
0010.00            K ITMNUM
*************** End of data ******************************
```

4.   Press **F3** to exit the SEU Edit screen and from the Exit screen save the DDS.

5.   Go to the Work with Members screen and compile ITEM.

6.   Enter the following DDS into ITBATCAR:

```
*************** Beginning of data ********************************
0001.00    *     THIS IS THE LOGICAL FILE FOR THE JOIN OF THE BATCH, CARTON,
0002.00    *     AND ITEM FILES
0003.00                              UNIQUE
0004.00            R ITBATCARFT      JFILE(YOURLIBXX/CARTON +
0005.00                                    YOURLIBXX/BATCH +
0006.00                                    YOURLIBXX/ITEM)
0007.00                              TEXT('LOGICAL CARTON')
0008.00            J                 JOIN(1 2)
0009.00                              JFLD(BCHNUM BCHNUM)
0010.00            J                 JOIN(2 3)
0011.00                              JFLD(ITMNUM ITMNUM)
0012.00              CRTNUM
0013.00              ITMNAM
0014.00              EXPDTE
0015.00              STORE
0016.00            K CRTNUM
*************** End of data ******************************
```

7.   Save and compile the member. A new logical file, ITBATCAR, will be created that contains the carton number and store number from CARTON, the type of milk in the carton from ITEM, and the carton's expiration date from BATCH.

Notice the two join specifications and JFLD keywords that were required to join the three files. The CARTON and BATCH files were linked by their shared field of BCHNUM, and then the correct ITEM record was linked through ITMNUM, the field ITEM shares with BATCH. Also notice that the join fields do not have to have field level specifications. Even though the join fields are used to create the logical file, they are not included in the file definition. The join fields are just used to build the access path to the data. No information contained in the join fields can be accessed through the logical file because the join fields do not have field level specifications.

## REVIEW QUESTIONS

1.   Why is DDS the primary data definition tool on the AS/400?

2.   What is a DDL? A DML?

3.   Explain the relationship between logical and physical files.

4.  Explain the relationship between logical files, source physical file members with a type of LF, and data physical file members with no type.

5.  What is the difference between file, record, and field specifications? Give a keyword function example that is available at each level.

6.  What advantages are there to including edits and audits in the file definition rather than the application programs?

7.  What are the modes that a DFU-generated update program can work in?

8.  What are the disadvantages of using DFU-generated update programs for large quantities of data?

**DISCUSSION QUESTIONS**

1.  Discuss the advantages of externally described files over internally described files.

2.  What are the advantages and disadvantages to using DFU versus a user-written application program to update files on the AS/400?

# *Security*

**7**

## Overview

This chapter explores security on the AS/400 and explains how to control access to data, programs, and system functions. The chapter will cover user profiles and authorization lists and show how they provide these functions.

After finishing this chapter, you will understand:

- Different authorities that can be defined for objects
- The purpose of authorization lists
- The purpose of a user profile and the information it contains

You also will be able to:

- Display and modify an object's authorization list
- Change your user profile

# Object Security

In most computer systems, access controls are supplied through the operating system, the database management system, and specialized security programs. The AS/400 is no exception. Its controls are provided through the combined DBMS and OS/400 operating system and can be accessed through a set of specialized CL commands.

Providing access to data and functions, however, is not a simple yes or no condition. Controls need to be exercised at many different levels for both data and functions. For instance, a user may need access to a function (change time card information) but should be able to use it only on certain data (his or her work hours). Or a user may need access to an entire file but should be able to perform only a limited set of functions against that file (like read and copy the file but not delete it).

To provide different levels of control, each object on the AS/400 has an *authorization list* associated with it. The authorization list contains the list of userids that can access the object and the functions each can perform. Whenever anyone tries to access an object, the operating system first checks the authorization list to make sure the person requesting the object is allowed to use it. If he or she is not allowed to access or perform a particular function against the object, the operating system will stop the user.

An authorization list is created for an object when the object is created and the person who creates the object is automatically given the highest level of authority, *ALL.

To view and change an object's authority, use the EDTOBJAUT (edit object authority) command. (The authorization to an object can also be edited from the Work with Objects screen by choosing option 2.) Specifying **EDTOBJAUT** for Object MASTODON in Library DINOSAUR, pressing ENTER and then F11 would result in the screen shown in Figure 7.1.

**FIGURE 7.1**

```
                        Edit Object Authority

Object. . . . . . . :   MASTODON    Object type . . . : *FILE
    Library . . . . . :   DINOSAUR   Owner . . . . . . : INTRO99

Type changes to current authorities, press Enter.

    Object secured by authorization list . . . . . . . .  *NONE__

            Object    -----Object----  ----------Data-----------
User      Authority  Opr  Mgt  Exist  Read  Add  Update  Delete
INTRO99   *ALL_____   X    X     X      X    X      X       X
*PUBLIC   *CHANGE__   X    _     _      X    X      X       X




                                                          Bottom
F3=Exit F5=Refresh     F6=Add new users  F10=Grant with reference object
F11=Nondisplay detail  F12=Cancel        F17=Top   F18=Bottom
```

Notice that another userid besides INTRO99 is listed. Depending on how your AS/400 was initialized, *PUBLIC and its authority may be included in your authorization list. *PUBLIC specifies what all AS/400 users can do with this object. In this case, everyone is given change authority, which means they can read, add, update, or delete the contents of the object. To change the public access, you can either type in another object authority keyword (like *EXCLUDE) or simply place an X under the functions you would like the userids to have. Blanking out all the Xs will result in denying access to the object for all users not explicitly identified in the authorization list.

The meaning of each of the object control authorities is as follows:

- **OBJOPR** (object operational authority). Allows content control authorities (read, add, and so on) to be specified. It also allows viewing of the object's description.

- **OBJMGT** (object management authority). Allows a user to move and rename the object.

- **OBJEXIST** (object existence authority). Allows a user to delete, save, and transfer ownership of an object.

For content control functions (in conjunction with OBJOPR authority), the following can be specified:

- **READ.** Enables the user to look at members in a source file.

- **ADD.** Allows the user to insert new information.

- **UPDATE.** Lets the user modify existing information.

- **DELETE.** Allows information to be erased.

The other object authority keywords that can be specified provide a combination of content control and object control functions:

- **EXCLUDE.** Denies all access to the object (denies file level access).

- **USE.** Gives object control (OBJOPR) and read function control.

- **CHANGE.** Gives object control and all content function control.

- **ALL.** Gives object MGT, OPR, and EXIST control and all content function control.

Userids can be added by pressing F6 at the Edit Object Authority screen. A new screen will be provided where userids can be typed. After entering the userids and pressing ENTER, you will be returned to the Edit Object Authority screen where the new userids will be displayed. The authority for each userid can be specified as described earlier.

Another way to add users is through the GRTOBJAUT (grant object authority) command. The syntax for the GRTOBJAUT command is as follows:

```
GRTOBJAUT OBJ(libname/objname) OBJTYPE(objtype)
USER(userid) AUT (up to eight of the preceding
values)
```

Executing this command provides the access specified in the AUT parameter to the object specified in the OBJ and OBJTYPE parameters for the signon id specified in the USER parameter.

Since all programs and data files are either objects or members contained within objects, access to them can be controlled through object authority. Functional control can be achieved by allowing access to or excluding users from program objects. For instance, if you want someone to be able to run a program but not change the source code, grant the user authority to the *PGM object but exclude him or her from the source physical file object that contains the source code members. (Denying access to an object denies access to the object's members.)

Object authority and logical files can be used to achieve record and field level control over data. Logical files can be created to include only a subset of fields or records. By granting authority to logical files, the user will be able to access only the fields and records as defined in the logical files.

Through object security, the AS/400 provides the capability to control access to any user-created programs and maintain file, record, or field level control over data.

The AS/400 also provides further functional control by controlling the system functions that a userid can perform. This is done by assigning special authorities to a userid or defining a userid as a particular class of userid. This information is stored in a new type of object called a user profile.

## Profiles

Every signon id has a whole series of system information associated with it—its password, the initial menu to be displayed, the initial program to be called, and so on (Figure 7.2). This userid-related data is called a user profile.

**FIGURE 7.2**

```
                    Create User Profile (CRTUSRPRF)

 Type choices, press Enter.

 User profile . . . . . . . .  JOEUSER   Name
 User password  . . . . . . .  RAITT     Name, *USRPRF, *NONE
 Set password to expired. . .  *YES      *NO, *YES
 Status . . . . . . . . . . .  *ENABLED  *ENABLED, *DISABLED
 User class . . . . . . . . .  *USER     *USER, *SYSOPR, *PGMR...
 Assistance level . . . . . .  *SYSVAL   *SYSVAL, *BASIC, *INTERMED...
 Current library  . . . . . .  *CRTDFT   Name, *CRTDFT
 Initial program to call  . .  *NONE     Name, *NONE
   Library  . . . . . . . . .            Name, *LIBL, *CURLIB
 Initial menu . . . . . . . .  MAIN      Name, *SIGNOFF
   Library  . . . . . . . . .    *LIBL   Name, *LIBL, *CURLIB
 Limit capabilities . . . . .  *NO       *NO, *PARTIAL, *YES
 Text 'description' . . . . .  *BLANK

                                                            Bottom
 F3=Exit F4=Prompt F5=Refresh F10=Additional parameters F12=Cancel
 F13=How to use this display  F24=More keys
 Parameter USRPRF required.
```

Each userid can be assigned access to predefined groups of AS/400 system functions. These groups of functions fall along system function lines (for example, one group contains all the security functions) or according to a user's job type (for example, another group contains all the system functions programmers would need to perform their jobs). The system function groups are assigned through a userid's *special authorities* parameter, and the job groups are assigned through the *user class* parameter. A series of special authority and class type values can be specified in the special authority and user class parameters.

## Special Authorities

As mentioned, groups of system functions can be specified in the Special authority parameter of the signon id's profile (Figure 7.3). The functional authority granted through these values are more closely in line with system organization than user needs. Some examples are:

- **\*SPLCTL.** Grants access to all spooling functions.

- **\*SECADM.** Would allow access to all security functions.

- **\*SAVSYS.** Lets a user save and restore all objects on the system.

- **\*JOBCTL.** Allows an id to hold, release, cancel, or clear all jobs.

**FIGURE 7.3**

```
                    Change User Profile (CHGUSRPRF)

Type choices, press Enter.
                    Additional Parameters

Special authority . . . . . .   *ALLOBJ   *SAME, *USRCLS, *NONE...
                                *JOBCTL
                                *SAVSYS
                                *SECADM
                                *SERVICE
                                *SPLCTL
Special environment . . . . .   *SYSVAL   *SAME, *SYSVAL, *NONE, *S36
Display sign-on information .    *SYSVAL   *SAME, *NO, *YES, *SYSVAL
Password expiration interval.   *SYSVAL   1-366, *SAME, *SYSVAL, *NOMAX
Limit device sessions . . . .   *SYSVAL   *SAME, *NO, *YES, *SYSVAL
Keyboard buffering  . . . . .   *SYSVAL   *SAME, *SYSVAL, *NO...
Maximum allowed storage . . .   *NOMAX    Kilobytes, *SAME, *NOMAX
Highest schedule priority . .   3         0-9, *SAME

                                                              More...
F3=Exit F4=Prompt F5=Refresh F12=Cancel F13=How to use this display
F24=More keys
```

Special authorities allow the userid to perform groups of functionally related CL commands. If system functions are to be assigned according to the user's job, then the value *USRCLS needs to be entered in the Special authority parameter, and one of the following user *class types* must be specified in the User class parameter.

## Class Types

Most organizations have a security officer who is responsible for controlling access to the system, data, and functions. One of the security officer's functions is to create signon ids for users and to define the associated profile parameters. A special userid, QSECOFR, has this capability. The ability to perform security functions comes from the class type defined for the QSECOFR id. The QSECOFR id's class type is *SECOFR (Figure 7.4). Having a class of *SECOFR allows the id to perform all the special authorities previously mentioned and more. For instance, some CL commands covered by the *SECOFR special authority are CRTUSRPRF (create user profile) and CHGUSRPRF (change user profile). Userids with *SECOFR authority can issue these commands for any userid.

This is as opposed to the CHGPRF (change profile) command. Everyone can use the CHGPRF command because everyone needs to be able to change his or her own profile. Prove this by using the CHGPRF command to change the initial program parameter in your profile. Change the initial program parameter to INITPGM, the program created in Chapter 3. Changes to a profile are put into effect only after the session ends and the user signs on again. So, after changing the initial program parameter, sign off the system. When you sign back on, PDM should be immediately started. Check that the current library has been changed as specified in INITPGM. Do this by choosing the Work with libraries option from the PDM menu and see what library name is filled in at the prompt. If the profile was updated correctly, it should be the library defined in INITPGM.

QSECOFR can perform these profile functions on all profiles. This is accomplished through object control. Each profile is an object. All signon ids are given access to their profile object. QSECOFR, however, by having a class type of *SECOFR, can access all objects, including every user's profile on the system.

*SECADM (security administrator) is another class type. An id that has *SECADM as its class can access the systems security

FIGURE 7.4

```
                      Change User Profile (CHGUSRPRF)

 Type choices, press Enter.

 User profile . . . . . . . > BIGSHOT     Name
 User password  . . . . . .   *SAME       Name, *SAME, *NONE
 Set password to expired  .   *NO         *SAME, *NO, *YES
 Status . . . . . . . . . .   *ENABLED    *SAME, *ENABLED, *DISABLED
 User class . . . . . . . .   *SECOFR     *SAME, *USER, *SYSOPR...
 Assistance level . . . . .   *SYSVAL     *SAME, *SYSVAL, *BASIC...
 Current library  . . . . .   *CRTDFT     Name, *SAME, *CRTDFT
 Initial program to call. .   INITPGM     Name, *SAME, *NONE
   Library. . . . . . . . .   QGPL        Name, *LIBL, *CURLIB
 Initial menu . . . . . . .   MAIN        Name, *SAME, *SIGNOFF
   Library. . . . . . . . .     *LIBL     Name, *LIBL, *CURLIB
 Limit capabilities . . . .   *NO         *SAME, *NO, *PARTIAL, *YES
 Text 'description' . . . .   'Security Administrator'

                                                                   More...
 F3=Exit F4=Prompt F5=Refresh F12=Cancel F13=How to use this display
 F24=More keys
```

functions—create and change profiles, change authorization lists, change passwords, and so on. By creating other ids with a class of *SECADM, the security officer does not have to perform all security tasks. These *SECADM ids enable the QSECOFR to distribute some of the system security work.

*USER class provides no special authorities. An id defined with a class of *USER can access and edit objects for which it has ownership.

*PGMR and *SYSOPR provide access to system functions regarding saving objects and job control. For instance, these classes allow a user to compile and run programs or cancel programs that are running. In general, the AS/400 developers created these class types to make it easier to grant authority to the system functions that are most likely to be used by programmers and system operators.

If the class types had not been created, the alternative would be authorizing each new programmer's and system operator's userid to the particular system functions needed. This would have been very time consuming.

## Summary

The AS/400 provides extensive functional and data level control capabilities. Through its object-oriented approach, it is able to provide access control to multiple levels of data, system functions, and user applications. Though most systems provide this, the AS/400's object-oriented architecture—treating all data and programs as objects—allows control through the same command set and utilities. Normally, there are separate commands, functions, and systems for data versus program control. For instance, most systems require separate database commands if record or field level control is needed.

The AS/400 architecture also provides several methods to easily grant system functions. The easiest is by specifying values for the user profile's user class and special authority parameters.

As with most commands and functions, the security and authorization functions are supported with prompts, screens, and on-line help to facilitate their use and understanding. All security functions can be accessed through either the associated CL commands or the extensive menu system.

## LAB EXERCISE

In this lab exercise, you will change the authorization list for the source physical file created earlier, INVSRC in YOURLIBXX.

1.  Grant authority to another user by typing the following at any command line and pressing ENTER. (Substitute someone else's userid for INTROXX in the USER keyword.)
    **GRTOBJAUT OBJ(YOURLIBXX/INVSRC) OBJTYPE(*FILE) USER(INTROXX) AUT(*USE)**

2.  Type **EDTOBJAUT** at the command line and press F4.

3.  At the Edit Object Authority (EDTOBJAUT) screen, enter **YOURLIBXX**, **INVSRC**, and ***FILE** at the appropriate prompts.

4.    At the Edit Object Authority screen, notice that the userid specified in the GRTOBJAUT command is in the authorization list.

5.    Press F11 for more detail on each userid's authority. For instance, notice that the *USE authority just granted comprises OBJOPR and READ authority.

6.    Delete the userid (just entered through the GRTOBJAUT command) by blanking out all X's under the various heading and press ENTER.

7.    Change the *PUBLIC authority by blanking out all the Xs under the various authority headings and press ENTER.

8.    Notice that by not granting OBJOPR, OBJMGT, and OBJEXIST, the special authority of *EXCLUDE has been defined. Other users cannot access your INVSRC file.

## REVIEW QUESTIONS

1.    Who has object authority?

2.    What is an authorization list?

3.    Explain how logical files help with data control.

4.    When is a user profile created, and what is its purpose?

5.    Explain the differences and similarities between special authorities and a user class.

6.    How are user-written applications and functions controlled on the AS/400?

7.    Describe the scope of authority granted to the QSECOFR userid.

8.    What object does the EDTOBJAUT command allow a user to modify?

## DISCUSSION QUESTIONS

1.    Explain the different levels of data control, and give reasons why each level would be needed.

2.    You are opening up a computer dating service using an AS/400. All your customers are very concerned with the confidentiality of the information they are supplying. Allay their fears by explaining how the AS/400 controls access to data and how access can be granted only to people they authorize.

# Scheduling and Monitoring Jobs

## Overview

This appendix explores the options available for running jobs on the system and explains the concept of subsystems. In addition, several new CL commands that allow users to schedule jobs for future execution and check the status of submitted jobs will be covered.

After finfishing this appendix, you will understand:

- Job queues
- AS/400 subsystems
- Interactive versus batch execution of programs

You also will be able to:

- Display jobs in specific subsystems
- Schedule and verify jobs on the batch subsystem

## Monitoring Jobs

Have you ever noticed the message when a program is compiled? The message states that the job has been submitted to the batch job queue. There are two ways programs can be run: interactively or in batch. When a user issues a CALL command or runs a job from a system screen, the program is executed *interactively*, meaning that the program can send or receive information from the display. Programs run in *batch* execute with no terminal interaction. For instance, compiling a program doesn't require any information from the terminal, so it is run in batch. That is why the program is submitted to the *batch* job queue. The question now becomes what is a job queue?

If you have compiled many programs, you may have noticed that the amount of time the compiling takes can vary. This is often due to the system load. If many programs are to be run, the jobs can back up, waiting to be executed.

When a program is submitted, the request to execute the program initially goes to a *job queue*. Job queues hold work requests and are associated with *subsystems*. An AS/400's resources are divided into pieces or subsystems; that is, the AS/400 allocates the CPU's time, main memory, and so forth, by subsystem. For instance, jobs submitted to the batch subsystem may have a lower priority than jobs submitted to the interactive subsystem (or vice versa). The CPU might work on all the jobs in the interactive job queue first and then work on the jobs in the batch job queue. When a user submits a compile, the compile job request goes to the batch job queue. Based on how the subsystems are defined, the job will wait on the job queue until the CPU becomes available.

Users can monitor the progress of their jobs by checking the batch job queue with the WRKJOBQ command. Within this command the job queue associated with the batch subsystem must be specified. This is done by typing **WRKJOBQ JOBQ(QGPL/QBATCH)**. This will result in the screen shown in Figure A.1 where the status of each job can be seen.

**FIGURE A.1**

```
                      Work with Job Queue

 Queue: QBATCH       Library: QGPL                    Status: RLS/SBS

 Type options, press Enter.
   2=Change    3=Hold    4=End    5=Work with    6=Release

 Opt     Job            User         Number        Priority     Status
   _     QDFTJOBD       COP1707      051574           5          SCD
   _     QDFTJOBD       COP1707      051575           5          SCD
   _     QDFTJOBD       INTRO99      051578           5          SCD




                                                              Bottom
 Parameters for options 2, 3 or command
 ===>
 F3=Exit    F4=Prompt    F6=Submit job    F12=Cancel    F21=Subsystem
 F22=Work with job schedule entries    F24=More keys
```

The `Work with Job Queue` screen (see Figure A.1) shows a list of jobs that have a status of `SCD` (scheduled), meaning they will sit in the job queue until their scheduled date and time arrive. If a submitted job isn't shown, it has probably already been executed. Jobs that are currently being executed can be checked through the WRKACTJOB (work with active jobs) command. For instance, specifying **WRKACTJOB SBS(QBATCH)** would result in the screen shown in Figure A.2, a display of all active jobs in the batch subsystem. On the `Work with Active Jobs` screen, notice that a CL program called CLPGM is being compiled. You can tell it is being compiled by the function listed. CRTCLPGM is the CL command that compiles a CL source member. Also notice that the job is taking up a minuscule .1 percent of the CPU. The top of the screen displays systemwide statistics on the total CPU usage and the number of active jobs across all subsystems.

**FIGURE A.2**

```
                       Work with Active Jobs
                                            03/04/93  11:25:52
      CPU %:    21.4      Elapsed time:   00:04:21     Active jobs: 56

      Type options, press Enter.
        2=Change  3=Hold  4=End   5=Work with  6=Release  7=Display message
        8=Work with spooled files 13=Disconnect ...

      Opt  Subsystem/Job  User      Type   CPU %  Function       Status
      __    QBATCH         QSYS      SBS     .1                   DEQW
      __      CLPGM        INTRO99   BCH     .1    CMD-CRTCLPGM   RUN




                                                             Bottom
      Parameters or command
      ===>_____
      F3=Exit    F5=Refresh   F10=Restart statistics F11=Display elapsed data
      F12=Cancel F23=More options   F24=More keys
```

To look at the current status of interactive jobs, type **WRKACTJOB SBS(QINTER)**. This will show you all the userids that are currently signed onto the AS/400 and the functions they are performing. Figure A.3 shows an example. Notice that your own id (INTRO99) shows up and that the function is WRKACTJOB. The other examples in Figure A.3 show two users (INTRO06 and INTRO01) currently logged on. INTRO06 is working with the interactive subsystem JOBQ, and INTRO01 is at the MAIN menu.

A number of other operations can also be performed from these monitoring screens. For instance, active jobs can be disconnected (users will be logged off) or jobs can be put on hold. To perform these operations, you have to be authorized to do so by the security administrator. (The special authority parameter that permits a user to perform these job functions is JOBCTL.)

FIGURE A.3

```
                        Work with Active Jobs
                                              03/04/93 11:19:45
   CPU %:   13.3   Elapsed time:   00:03:38   Active jobs:   55

   Type options, press Enter.
     2=Change  3=Hold  4=End  5=Work with  6=Release  7=Display message
     8=Work with spooled files 13=Disconnect ...

   Opt  Subsystem/Job  User    Type  CPU %  Function      Status
    __   QINTER        QSYS    SBS    .0                  DEQW
    __    DSP07        INTRO06 INT    .0    CMD-WRKJOBQ    DSPW
    __    DSP18        INTRO01 INT    .0    MNU-MAIN       DSPW
    __    DSP99        INTRO99 INT    1.8   CMD-WRKACTJOB  RUN



                                                          Bottom
   Parameters or command
   ===>_____
   F3=Exit    F5=Refresh  F10=Restart statistics  F11=Display elapsed data
   F12=Cancel F23=More options  F24=More keys
```

## Scheduling Jobs

Programs can also be scheduled to run on specific days and at specific times. This is done with the SBMJOB (submit job) command. The submit job command allows the user to specify a discrete date such as 1/23/96 or relative dates such as *MONTHEND or *WED. Using the relative dates will result in the job being added to the batch job queue with a discrete date of execution, for example, a discrete date for the last day of the current month or the next Wednesday.

A job's scheduled date can be shown by first displaying the batch job queue (as in Figure A.1) and then selecting option 5. The scheduled date and time of execution will be displayed (Figure A.4) as

FIGURE A.4

```
                    Display Job Status Attributes
                                                    System:
   Job:  QDFTJOBD     User:  INTRO99         Number: 051578
   Status of job. . . . . . . . . . . . . . . . . :  SCD
   Entered system:
     Date . . . . . . . . . . . . . . . . . . . . :  03/04/93
     Time . . . . . . . . . . . . . . . . . . . . :  11:38:11
   Scheduled:
     Date . . . . . . . . . . . . . . . . . . . . :  01/23/96
     Time . . . . . . . . . . . . . . . . . . . . :  11:38:11
   Started:
     Date . . . . . . . . . . . . . . . . . . . . :
     Time . . . . . . . . . . . . . . . . . . . . :
   Subsystem. . . . . . . . . . . . . . . . . . . :
     Subsystem pool ID. . . . . . . . . . . . . . :

                                                    More...
   Press Enter to continue.
   F3=Exit    F5=Refresh    F12=Cancel    F16=Job menu
```

well as the date the job was added to the job queue. Note that the time of day when the job was scheduled and the time for execution on 1/23/96 are the same. This occurred because no time was specified in the SBMJOB command. The current time is used as the default.

## Summary

The AS/400 provides systemwide monitoring and scheduling of jobs. The SBMJOB command allows the user to schedule a program for execution on a certain day and at a specific time. Executing the SBMJOB command adds the specified program to the batch job queue, where it will reside until the scheduled date and time. The WRKJOBQ and WRKACTJOB commands allow the programmer to check on all scheduled jobs and look at the current jobs being executed in any subsystem.

# *Alternative Programming Environments*

# B

## Overview

This appendix covers alternative methods for executing common programming functions and how to tailor the PDM environment. The `Programmer Menu` and some advanced PDM functions will also be discussed.

After finishing this appendix, you will understand:

- The differences between the `Programmer Menu` and the PDM screens
- The advantages and disadvantages of executing programming-related commands through PDM options, the `Programmer Menu` options, and CL commands

You also will be able to:

- Execute programming functions from the `Programmer Menu`
- Create and execute user-defined options for PDM screens

## The Programmer Menu versus PDM

Whenever there is a lull in the conversation between AS/400 programmers, a sure-fire way of restarting the conversation is to advocate either the Programmer Menu or PDM as the best way to execute programming functions (compiling, editing, and so on). Some programmers will enumerate the faults of the chosen method and extol the virtues of the unchosen method, whereas others will laugh derisively and wonder out loud how anyone could possibly disagree. To establish yourself as an AS/400 programmer (and join in on this scholarly discussion), you should be acquainted with the Programmer Menu and its capabilities.

## Invoking and Using the Programmer Menu

From the AS/400 Main Menu choose option 5, Programming. This will bring up the Programming screen (Figure B.1). From this screen, you can invoke either Programming Development Manager (PDM) (option 2) or Programmer menu (option 1). Choose option 1 to display the Programmer Menu screen (Figure B.2).

The Programmer Menu offers some of the same functions as the PDM menus, such as editing a member or running a program. However, several options are available that provide easier access to some commonly used programmer utilities. For instance, selecting option 1 will result in the AS/400 Data File Utility (DFU) utility screen being displayed, and selecting option 9 will result in the AS/400 Screen Design Aid (SDA) screen being displayed. With PDM the user would have to access a screen with a command line, then issue the STRDFU or STRSDA command.

Several other functions are also easier to use from the Programmer Menu than from PDM. For instance, to edit a source member from the Programmer Menu, the programmer fills in four prompts and presses ENTER. The programmer would:

**FIGURE B.1**

```
PROGRAM                      Programming
                                               System: CHICAGO
Select one of the following:

     1. Programmer menu
     2. Programming Development Manager (PDM)
     3. Utilities
     4. Programming language debug
     5. Structured Query Language (SQL) pre-compiler
     6. Question and answer
     7. IBM product information
     8. Copy screen image
     9. Cross System Product/Application Execution (CSP/AE)

    50. System/36 programming

    70. Related commands

Selection or command
===>
F3=Exit  F4=Prompt  F9=Retrieve  F12=Cancel  F13=User support
F16=AS/400 Main menu
```

**FIGURE B.2**

```
                              Programmer Menu
                                                        System: CHICAGO
       Select one of the following:
            1. Start AS/400 Data File Utility
            2. Work with AS/400 Query
            3. Create an object from a source file    object name, type, pgm for CMD
            4. Call a program                         program name
            5. Run a command                          command
            6. Submit a job                           (job name), , ,(command)
            7. Go to a menu                           menu name
            8. Edit a source file member              (srcmbr),  (type)
            9. Design display format using SDA        (srcmbr), ,(mode)
           90. Sign off                               (*nolist, *list)

       Selection . . . . . __        Parm . . . . _____
       Type  . . . . . . . _____  Parm 2 . . . _____
       Command . . . . . . _____
       Source file . . . . _____   Source library . . . . . . . . *LIBL_____
       Object library  . . _____   Job description . . . . . . . . *USRPRF___

       F3=Exit       F4=Prompt            F6=Display messages    F10=Command entry
       F12=Cancel    F14=Work with submitted jobs                F18=Work with output
```

- Type **8** at the selection prompt on the `Programmer Menu`.

- Type the member name at the `Parm` prompt.

- Type the member's source physical file name at the `Source file` prompt.

- Type the member's library at the `Source library` prompt.

- Press ENTER.

SEU would be invoked for the specified member. When SEU is exited, the user will be returned to the `Programmer Menu`. To perform the same function on PDM, the user would have to:

- Choose the `Work with members` option from the `PDM Main Menu`.

- Fill in three prompts at the `Specify Members to Work With` screen:

  The member name at the `Member Name` prompt.

  The source physical file name at the `File` prompt.

  The library name at the `Library` prompt.

- Press ENTER.

- Choose option 2, `Edit`, on the `Work with Members Using PDM` screen.

- Press ENTER.

In this case, it seems that the `Programmer Menu` is easier to use than PDM. (Even invoking SEU from the command line seems more difficult than the `Programmer Menu` since it requires remembering the STRSEU command syntax and keywords.)

Besides paging through a series of screens in order to execute a command, PDM will often force the user to switch between screens to execute certain functions. The Programmer Menu, however, allows the user to execute many of the same functions from just one screen. For instance, to compile and run a program in PDM, you would start at the Work with Members Using PDM screen and specify option 14 next to the source member to be compiled. To run the program, the user would have to switch to the Work with Members Using PDM screen and specify the run option next to the program object just created.

With the Programmer Menu, a member can be compiled by choosing option 3 and specifying the source member (at the Parm prompt), member type (at the Type prompt), file (at the Source file prompt), and library (at the Source library prompt). The new program can then be run by choosing option 4 and specifying the program name (at the Parm prompt) and the library (at the Object library prompt).

When executing many of the programming functions (edit, call, submit, go, compile, and so on), the Programmer Menu is acting as a generic prompt screen. Its Parm and Parm 2 prompts are used to prompt for different information depending on the function executed. (Specific CL command prompt screens, however, can still be invoked from the Programmer Menu by typing the option number and pressing F4. A command line is also available for the programmer to specify any CL command.)

It seems that we have solved the argument and the Programmer Menu is the better way.

## Tailoring the PDM Environment

On many PDM screens, functions are executed by typing an option next to the library, object, or member. Each PDM screen has an area that displays the various system options available (copy, delete, display, and so on). In addition to the displayed options, the AS/400 allows a user to define option codes (provided the security officer has granted authority to access and change the option definitions). These user-defined option codes can be created to execute any CL command.

Press F24 to display more function keys and notice F16, the User options function. Pressing F16 will display a list of one- and two-character user-defined options that can be executed from the PDM screens (Figure B.3). Next to each option is the command that will be executed when the option is specified. These options are all user defined and can be modified.

Notice that the commands follow the normal CL command syntax rules; however, they seem to have some strange codes (&O, &L, &N, and the like) embedded within the command. These codes, called *substitution parameters*, are used to retrieve information from the PDM screen and include that information in the option command. For instance, option C calls a program. The program name and library are retrieved from the line on which the option is specified. Since compiling with PDM results in the program object name and the source member name being the same, this option could be specified on the Work with Members Using PDM screen, and the name of the member would be used as the name of the program to be called. In this way, a program created by *compiling* the source code member from the Work with Members Using PDM screen could also be *run* from the Work with Members Using PDM screen. The user-defined option eliminates the need to switch between PDM screens.

FIGURE B.3

```
                        Work with User-Defined Options

    File . . . . . . . : QAUOOPT         Member . . . . . . : QAUOOPT
      Library . . . . :   QGPL

    Type options, press Enter.
      2=Change           3=Copy           4=Delete         5=Display

    Opt Option   Command
     _    C      CALL &O/&N
     _    CF     CLRPFM &L/&N
     _    DM     DSPMSG
     _    ED     ENDDBG
     _    OF     SIGNOFF
     _    SF     STRDFU OPTION(2)
     _    SS     STRSDA OPTION(1)
     _    SP     WRKSPLF
     _    WQ     WRKOUTQ OUTQ
                                                             More...
    Command
    ===> _____
    F3=Exit         F4=Prompt          F5=Refresh      F6=Create
    F9=Retrieve     F10=Command entry                  F24=More keys
```

Besides making PDM easier to user, new options can be defined for the PDM screen that provide the functions available on the Programmer Menu (such as STRDFU and STRSDA). In addition, functions that aren't available on the Programmer Menu (or any other PDM screen) can be created. For instance, an option could be created to add a specified program to the DEBUG stack. Remember from Chapter 4 that one of the drawbacks of DEBUG is that it isn't tied into the PDM menu system. This can be overcome with user-defined options.

As an example, let's create SD, the option to add a program to the DEBUG stack. This will be a new function not available on any PDM screen or the Programmer Menu. In addition, this option will use substitution parameters to retrieve the program name from the screen.

The CL command to add a program to the DEBUG stack is STRDBG. We want to retrieve the name of the library and program to be added to the DEBUG stack from the screen. Two substitution parameters that will do this are &O and &N. &O retrieves the library name of the object or member at which the option is specified, and &N retrieves the name of the object or member at which the option is specified. (For a full list and explanation of all the substitution codes available, press F1, Help, at the Change User-Defined Option screen.)

If a user was at the Work with Objects Using PDM screen and typed SD next to a program, the library containing the program and the program name would be incorporated into the STRDBG command. If SD were typed next to a member on the Work with Members Using PDM screen, the member name and library it belonged to would be returned. Because source members and program objects share the same name in PDM, typing SD next to the source member would also identify the correct program object to add to the DEBUG stack.

All CL command parameters can be specified within the option definition. For instance, STRDBG has a parameter that controls whether production libraries should be updated while the program is in DEBUG. For our purposes, we will specify *YES.

To create the new option, press **F6** at the Work with User-Defined Options screen (Figure B.3), and the Create User-Defined Option screen (Figure B.4) will be displayed. Type the new option code and command as in Figure B.5 and press **ENTER**. The Work with User-Defined Options screen will be redisplayed, and SD will be in the list.

**FIGURE B.4**

```
                    Create User-Defined Option

Type option and command, press Enter.

  Option . . . . . . . . .  __ Option to create

  Command. . . . . . . .  _____
  _____
  _____
  _____




  F3=Exit      F4=Prompt      F12=Cancel
```

**FIGURE B.5**

```
                    Create User-Defined Option

Type option and command, press Enter.

  Option . . . . . . . . .  SD Option to create

  Command. . . . . . . .  STRDBG &O/&N UPDPROD(*YES)_____
  _____
  _____
  _____




  F3=Exit      F4=Prompt      F12=Cancel
```

## Summary

The AS/400 offers an alternative screen for programmers to work from called the Programmer Menu. It provides several functions not readily available from the PDM screens, such as options to invoke SDA and DFU. The Programmer Menu also offers the convenience of being able to execute many of the same functions as PDM but from a single screen. With PDM, users are often forced to switch between screens to execute certain functions; this is not the case with the Programmer Menu. PDM, however, does offer a significant advantage. It provides a method for users to create their own options. Users can define one- or two-character option codes that will execute any CL command. In addition, information can be retrieved from the PDM screen and embedded into the CL command to be executed. This gives the users the ability to tailor the AS/400 programming environment in any fashion desired.

The age-old question of which method is better has been raised. To promote peaceful relations among all AS/400 users, this author will take the Fifth and allow each user to choose his or her own way.

# *Index*